Your Obedient Servant

A Comedy by

Diana Morgan

based on an idea by Dorothea Gotfurt

Evans Plays London

This Edition
Dedicated with Gratitude
to
Patrick Hampshire.

0-237-49144-3

3603789154

Printed in Great Britain by
Lewis Reprints Limited, London and Tonbridge

237 49144 3   PR 1575

Your Obedient Servant

This play was first presented at the Richmond Theatre, on 17th August 1959, with the following cast:—

LAURA PEMBERTON	*Margaret Ward*
MRS. PEMBERTON, her mother-in-law	*Winifred Evans*
CAROLINE PEMBERTON ⎱ her daughters ⎰	*Pauline Stroud*
JULIA PEMBERTON ⎰	*Janice Edgard*
CHARLES SELBY	*Derek Bond*
EDWARD LLEWELLYN	*Walter Horsbrugh*

Décor by JOHN PIPER *and directed by* JACK WILLIAMS

The action takes place in the living-room of LAURA PEMBERTON's *flat off Campden Hill. Time: the present.*

ACT ONE

SCENE 1	An afternoon in April
SCENE 2	Afternoon, a week later

ACT TWO

Saturday afternoon, a few days later

ACT THREE

Saturday morning, a week later

No character, in this play, is intended to represent any person, alive or dead.

NOTE: *Running time of this play, excluding intervals, is approximately one hour and forty-seven minutes.*

PRODUCTION NOTE

ALTHOUGH *Your Obedient Servant* is primarily a comedy and contains—
I hope!—several comedy situations which can be played for all they
are worth, it remains a comedy and not a farce. In other words, I have
tried to make the characters recognizable as people you might con-
ceivably meet at any moment—living people to whom something
slightly unusual happens in the ordinary course of their lives rather
than puppets to whom *extra*ordinary things go on happening for the
whole of three acts.

This is not to disparage good farce, nor the creators of it. Far from
it: I have the greatest admiration for this most difficult of all theatrical
forms and for those who practise it successfully. I just know that I
can't write it myself and that I certainly haven't attempted to here.

What I *have* tried to do is to mingle the ludicrous with the tender and
touching and, in the event, it proved that the formula worked. It
should always work, provided that the sincere scenes are played with
sincerity and with the remembrance that it not only isn't necessary—it
is positively destructive—for a comedy to provide a continuous bar-
rage of bellylaughs. Smiles, even occasional wry ones, can give as much
pleasure in the theatre as aching ribs. And the successful alternation of
scenes which gain your sympathy with those that make you laugh is the
ambition of all practical playwrights.

Now, with that general essay off my chest, let me get down to
details. The setting and atmosphere of *Your Obedient Servant* is that of
the class known alternatively as Upper-Middle or Professional.
Every character is either doing, has done, or hopes soon to be doing
a job of work. These are not the idle rich: they are the industrious near-
poor. Not particularly keen on money, except as a means to an end,
they are all passionately interested in their careers, whether these take
place in archaeology, show business, or the creation of a home with
steady, worth-while values.

LAURA is the most important character in the play. She may seem
scatter-brained and untidy, yet she is quick to spot the value of objects
she knows about and her taste, in things or people, is always sure.
Widowed young, she badly needs a man about the house, particularly
one who can control and guide her children for, like most mothers,
she doesn't always understand her daughters though she loves them

dearly and knows they love her in return. She wants to do what's best for them and, if in the end, her heart rules her head, who shall blame her? She is a very lovable and loving person.

CHARLES is essentially an actor, with all the genuine actor's attributes. An exhibitionist, he cannot resist an appreciative audience, for all his instincts and training have taught him to cajole them till they eat out of the hollow of his hand. He learns that this can lead to trouble in real life, when he can no longer resume his own private existence the moment the curtain falls, but he is big enough and kind enough to face this as a man and not as just a spotlit robot.

MRS. PEMBERTON is by no means the stock mother-in-law. When her son was alive, she was devoted to the daughter-in-law who made him happy, and is still devoted after his death, though she thoroughly disapproves of Laura's fecklessness without him and of her lack of control of the grandchildren. Laura must marry again, for everybody's sake, but Laura must be happy when she does so.

CAROLINE is passing through the most difficult of all feminine ages: the girl who is not quite yet a woman. *She'll* be all right: at the moment Art (with a capital "A") is ruling her life and she is so sophisticated (in theory) about the Cinema and the H-Bomb and Music and Sex that she hasn't had time for individual men, until one of them gives her quite a healthy jolt.

JULIA is less complex than Caroline, so far, being younger. But she'll develop on much the same lines. She might possibly come to love Films (or even TV?) as much as the Stage some day. Meanwhile, she'll continue learning the hard way about the basic human ingredients. We all wish her very well.

EDWARD. Happy in the cloistered life of Cambridge and the rarefied atmosphere of archaeology and the Athenaeum, Edward is far from being a pompous ass. Selfish and set in his ways, perhaps, like many a successful long-time bachelor, he yet has a genuine love for Laura and is bewildered and hurt when she finally turns him down. It is to his credit that he takes this with such dignity.

To sum up, *Your Obedient Servant* is a comedy—a *romantic* comedy.

DIANA MORGAN

CHARACTERS

in order of appearance

Laura Pemberton

Mrs. Pemberton

Caroline Pemberton

Julia Pemberton

Charles Selby

Edward Llewellyn

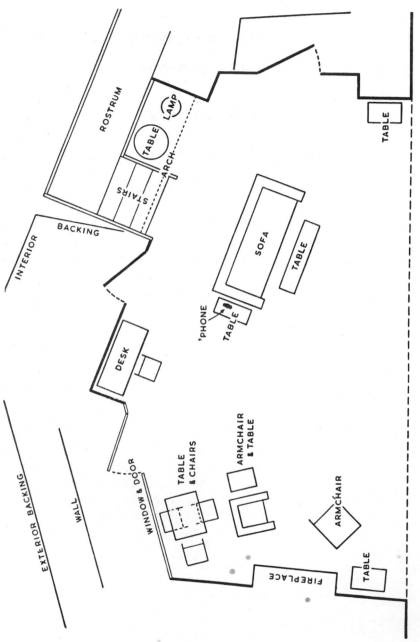

*YOUR OBEDIENT SERVANT

ACT ONE

SCENE I

The hall-cum-living-room of LAURA PEMBERTON's flat. This flat con-sists of the two top floors of an old house somewhere off Campden Hill. The room we see has the main door back stage L.C., and L. of that is the little staircase leading to the attic bedrooms. There is a door D.L. leading to the kitchen. U.R. and angled across the corner is a large studio window which opens out on to a narrow roof with a coping on which LAURA hopefully keeps window boxes. The furniture is good and comfortable, with a few surprisingly fine pieces and the china on the mantel-shelf D.R. is exquisite, but the whole room has an uncared-for air; books and papers lie about in confusion and there are the remains of a hurried meal on the table near the window. The time is about four o'clock on a spring afternoon.

As the curtain rises, there is a scrabbling at the front door, and it eventually bursts open. LAURA enters, followed by her mother-in-law, MRS. PEMBERTON. LAURA is in her late thirties, vague and quite enchanting. MRS. PEMBERTON wears a downright tweed coat and skirt and manner to match. LAURA is laden with carrier bags bulging with food. MRS. PEMBERTON carries a large and heavy gilt clock. The telephone starts to ring.

LAURA. Oh, dear! (She looks around desperately: there is nowhere she can park her belongings.) Talk about a shambles!

MRS. P. (indicating the telephone). Aren't you going to answer it?

LAURA. You know, if I don't get a daily woman soon . . . (To telephone.) All right: I'm coming!

(She moves towards it, depositing one bag of vegetables on the floor beside it. As she picks up the receiver, nearly tripping over the long and much tangled lead as she does so, the vegetables burst out of the bag and are neatly fielded by MRS. P., who has managed to park the clock.)

(At telephone.) Hello. Yes, Mrs. Pemberton speaking. Yes. (To MRS. P.) It's the Campden Hill Domestic Agency. (At telephone.) Oh, hello, Miss Benson—have you found me anybody? Oh dear, no one at all? I'm quite desperate, Miss Benson. You see, I'm at my shop all day and. . . . Yes. . . . Thank you. Good-bye. (*She hangs up.*) Blast the woman! She promised. She's the one that got me Gladys.

MRS. P. Was Gladys the one who stole your stockings and swore at you?

LAURA (*disentangling herself from the telephone*). That was Mrs. Potts. Gladys was the one who got religion and prayed at me. Oh dear, what am I going to do?

MRS. P. It's all Nannie's fault—first she spoilt you and then she completely ruined the girls.

LAURA. And to get married like that—to a man she met on the top of a thirty-one bus! Imagine Nannie allowing herself to be picked up.

MRS. P. Perhaps she did the picking.

LAURA. Oh no—I know the dialogue by heart. He said, "Is this right for Church Street?" And she said "Yes" and he said "Haven't we met before?" and she said "No" and then he said "Well, we have now, so what about it?"

MRS. P. I must say I'd never have imagined Nannie the type to inspire love at first sight. I always thought she looked like a melancholy horse.

LAURA. Maybe that's what attracted him—he drives a van for the R.S.P.C.A.

MRS. P. How long since she left?

LAURA. About four weeks. Then I had Mrs. Potts for two days and dear Gladys for three.

MRS. P. And now nobody.

LAURA. Less than nobody.

MRS. P. (*who has been doing a little tidying*). You know, you and the girls ought to be able to manage this flat between you. Don't they do anything?

LAURA. They make their beds.

MRS. P. So I should hope. What else?

LAURA. Well, Caroline gets the coffee and . . .

(*The telephone rings again.* LAURA *picks up the receiver.*)

(*At telephone.*) Hello. Yes, this is Mrs. Pemberton. Yes, I'll hold on. (*To* MRS. P.) This is another agency—they promised to ring me if there was any hope, or even if there wasn't. (*At telephone.*) Oh, good afternoon—have you been able to find me anyone? Not even an Italian? Yes. . . . Yes, I'm sure you have a waiting list as long as your arm. Yes. Good-bye. (*She hangs up.*) And d'you know what *they* call themselves? "The Housewife's Friend!"

MRS. P. (*taking a deep breath*). Laura, I must speak to you seriously.

LAURA. Why do people always say "seriously" when they mean "disapprovingly"?

MRS. P. You are my favourite daughter-in-law.

LAURA. Oh, goody!

MRS. P. You made George very happy.

LAURA. Poor darling! He made me very happy, too.

MRS. P. But you're hopeless where the girls are concerned. You spoil them appallingly. What they need is a firm hand. Laura, you ought to marry Edward Llewellyn.

LAURA. Would you say Edward had a firm hand?

MRS. P. Firm enough.

LAURA. Have you noticed how red they are? I suppose it's all that digging. Did you see in *The Times* yesterday that he's found another dreary old burial urn somewhere?

MRS. P. Laura, don't change the subject.

LAURA. I'm not. I'm talking about Edward's hands.

MRS. P. You know perfectly well what I mean. Anyway, you ought to marry again for your own sake. You're the sort of woman who needs a husband.

LAURA. Darling, aren't you sweet! Lots of mothers-in-law would simply hate the idea!

MRS. P. I'm sure George, wherever he is, must be very worried at the thought of you without a man to take care of you.

LAURA. He always used to say that if anything happened to him he'd want me to marry again immediately.

MRS. P. You see.

LAURA. *He* said I needed a keeper!

MRS. P. Exactly what I said.

LAURA. Only you put it more elegantly.

MRS. P. And Edward's very well off—you could give up the shop.

LAURA. But I love the shop!

MRS. P. There's no real money in antiques these days—the Americans have got far too knowing. No, you could give up the shop and I could keep on going to sales and sell the stuff privately.

LAURA. Perhaps Edward doesn't want to marry me.

MRS. P. Nonsense, he's devoted to you!

LAURA. If you ask me, Edward's very comfortable as he is with that Mrs. Sandham of his. She's a wonderful housekeeper. Goodness, that reminds me. (*She rummages in her bag and produces a piece of paper.*) Nancy Meadowes came into the shop today—didn't buy anything, but she gave me the telephone number of another agency who'd found someone for Lady Bristowe. (*She dials.*) It's called "Service for Ladies". (*At telephone.*) Hello? Is that "Service for Ladies"? (*To* MRS. P.) Such a nice voice. (*At telephone.*) Hello, this is Mrs. Pemberton of seventeen Carrington Gardens. I hear you found someone wonderful for Lady Bristowe. Yes, I want a help urgently. There's not a great deal of work. (MRS. P. *raises her eyes to heaven.*) I'm out all day and so are my daughters. We just want somebody reliable who'll clean, and prepare the meals and, well, generally take charge. What! You can? Oh, yes, I'm sure we could come to terms. As soon as possible? . Thank you. I'm most terribly grateful! Good-bye. (*She hangs up.*) They're sending a help round as soon as possible. (*Once again she has to disentangle herself from the cord.*)

MRS. P. When's that? Next week?

LAURA. This afternoon! Isn't it wonderful?

MRS. P. Don't be too optimistic—she'll probably be quite hopeless.

LAURA. Wouldn't it be simply splendid if she turned out to be a treasure?

MRS. P. Treasures went out with basement kitchens and Queen Victoria.

LAURA (*crossing to kitchen*). What we need is a delicious cup of tea to celebrate. (*She opens the kitchen door, and stands dismayed.*) Oh dear.

MRS. P. (*looking over her shoulder*). It looks like the morning after Mafeking.

LAURA. Julia must have come home to lunch.

(*She goes into the kitchen.* MRS. P. *picks up the clock and places it on the mantelshelf.*)

MRS. P. (*calling*). Now don't let this clock go for a penny under twelve pounds.

LAURA (*from kitchen*). I won't.

MRS. P. (*calling*). And I'll bring the rest of the stuff from the Mount-stephan sale when I come up next week.

(LAURA *appears in the kitchen doorway, a tea cloth in her hands.*)

LAURA. I had a man in this morning asking for a wine cooler. He—

(*The main door opens and* CAROLINE PEMBERTON *comes in. She is a pretty, intense girl of about seventeen. She is dressed in the full regalia of the Fulham Road intelligentsia—very tight scarlet and green drain-pipe trousers, yellow sweater, navy blue duffle coat, pink socks, light blue sandals, gold ear-rings and a mop of jagged hair. She has just started work for a minor Documentary Film Company.* LAURA *re-enters the kitchen.*)

CAROLINE (*kissing* MRS. P.). Hello, Grannie. (*Calling.*) Can I have tea at once, Mummy? I've got to hurry. I'm going to a party in the King's Road.

MRS. P. Like that?

CAROLINE. What's wrong?

MRS. P. Caroline, we all know you're a very intelligent girl, and what I can't understand is why an intelligent girl should wear such damnable clothes!

CAROLINE. Grannie!

MRS. P. What on earth is wrong with a pretty frock and well-brushed, clean hair?

CAROLINE (*indignantly*). My hair *is* clean.

MRS. P. It doesn't look it.

CAROLINE. I suppose you'd like me to be like those girls on the covers of women's magazines?

MRS. P. Why not?

CAROLINE. Don't you realize that as one appears one is? This is me, Caroline Pemberton, not a toothy technicolour doll bathing in ghastly uniformity and soulless mediocrity.

(LAURA *enters with a tea tray which she puts on the table.*)

LAURA. Remind me to get a new kettle sometime, someone. Talk about a kettle being furred—this one's positively "minked"!

CAROLINE. Mummy, Grannie is sounding off about my clothes again.

LAURA. Well, you do look pretty disgusting, darling. Here, give this cup to Grannie.

MRS. P. (*taking the cup from* CAROLINE). What will you do at this party of yours—dance?

CAROLINE (*coldly*). Ernest Fellowes, who worked with Alberti on "Gli uccelli Castrati", is going to talk about the Umbrian Cinema.

MRS. P. (*plaintively*). When I tell my friends I have a granddaughter who is in films they all ask which pictures and I never know.

LAURA. Oh, she edited a simply enthralling one about itinerant hop-pickers. (*To* CAROLINE.) What was it called, darling? (*To* MRS. P.) It was a documentary, you know.

MRS. P. I don't know.

LAURA. Oh, it's all true and sort of dimly lit and terribly badly acted because they have real people instead of actors. It's what they call Cinema as distinct from the Pictures.

(*Before* CAROLINE *can protest, the door is flung open and* JULIA *enters. She is a happy, healthy schoolgirl of maybe fifteen in a neat school uniform.*)

JULIA (*embracing* MRS. P.). Grannie! (*To* LAURA.) I just rushed in to say I'm going to tea with Susan—she's got the new L.P. of John Neville, lucky thing! She's going to put it on and we're going to sit in the dark and imagine that he's speaking to us alone. "Now is the winter of our discontent made glorious summer—"

LAURA (*interrupting*). What about your home-work?

JULIA (*ignoring this*). Bye, Grannie darling. (*To* LAURA.) Susan's waiting downstairs. Bye!

(*She runs out, slamming the door behind her.*)

LAURA (*to* MRS. P.). All her form are John Neville mad.

CAROLINE. That ham!

LAURA (*to* MRS. P.). She simply lives at the Old Vic. I'm terribly afraid she wants to be an actress.

MRS. P. You know, I think I'm glad I was born before girls all *had* to have careers—it was much more restful just to sit about and wait to get married.

LAURA. But if you didn't get married?

MRS. P. (*vaguely*). Oh, there was always church work or gardening. (*She rises.*) Well, good-bye, my dear. I hope the new help will live up to your expectations.

LAURA. Why don't you stay up and we'll have a little dinner at that Italian place?

MRS. P. No, I promised Richard I'd catch the five-fifteen. He's been a bit gouty lately and likes to be made a fuss of.

LAURA. Give him my love.

MRS. P. I will. Now, remember, not a penny less than twelve pounds for the clock. Good-bye, Caroline.

CAROLINE. I'm just going—I'll come with you.

MRS. P. Only as far as the front door—I don't want my friends to see me consorting with a wild woman of Borneo.

(She moves towards the door.)

CAROLINE. Bye, mother.

LAURA. Will you be late?

CAROLINE. Very probably.

(She goes out after MRS. P. and closes the door. Left alone, LAURA heaves a sigh. Then she crosses to the window and, opening it, steps out. The sky is turning pink and a thrush is heard. She stands there for a moment and then re-enters the room, closing the window. She crosses to the light switch by the mantel-shelf and turns it on. She then goes to the table and piles the cups and saucers on to the tray. The front door bell rings sharply. She nearly drops the tray but manages to save it, puts it down, crosses to the door and opens it. CHARLES SELBY stands on the threshold. He is a tall, good looking man. He wears a dark suit and an unobtrusive tie.)

CHARLES. Mrs. Pemberton?

LAURA. Yes.

CHARLES. Service for ladies.

LAURA. What?

CHARLES. I am the help from the "Service for ladies" Bureau, madam.

LAURA. But, you're a man!

CHARLES. Yes, madam.

LAURA. But—please come in.

CHARLES *(entering and closing the door)*. Thank you, madam.

LAURA. But, I don't understand—there must be some mistake—did they think I wanted a butler or something ridiculous like that?

CHARLES. Oh, no, madam—but all the helps at the bureau are men— mostly ex-servicemen.

LAURA. But I wanted someone who'll clean and—wash up and things like that.

CHARLES. That's all part of the service, madam.

LAURA. I'm sorry, but I'm afraid it's no good. I mean, I just wanted a woman—I mean, it's not worth your while.

CHARLES. Why not?

LAURA. Well, I couldn't pay you enough, for one thing.

CHARLES. It's the usual rate—seven shillings and sixpence an hour, or seven pounds a week if we live in.

LAURA. Live in?

CHARLES. Yes, madam. I presume you have accommodation?

LAURA. Well, yes, but—

CHARLES. I thought this flat looked roomy as well as attractive.

LAURA. But you can't get people to live in for love or money!

CHARLES. Well, personally I always prefer it. One becomes, so to speak, in tune with the household.

LAURA (*weakly*). You—you've been doing this long?

CHARLES. Some years, madam. During a Territorial Army exercise, I acted as batman to General Sir Archibald Ismay-Rotherhithe, and I grew attached as it were to the occupation. When he retired he asked me to look after him. I did.

LAURA. I suppose General Sir Archibald—er?

CHARLES. Ismay-Rotherhithe. A very gallant gentleman.

LAURA. I suppose he would give you a reference?

CHARLES. Unfortunately, madam, he is no longer with us. Cirrhosis of the liver.

LAURA. But if you've been used to generals and things like that—er, what's your name?

CHARLES. Charles, madam.

LAURA. Well, Charles, if you've been used to that sort of life, you'd be bored stiff here.

CHARLES. I beg to differ, madam.

LAURA. But you would. This is a very ordinary household. It's just me and my two daughters. We're out nearly all day. We never give dinner parties. We haven't any grand friends or anything.

CHARLES. The General lived in the strictest retirement, madam, after publishing his memoirs. He was not on speaking terms with any of his acquaintances.

LAURA. I'm sorry, but I'm afraid I don't think you'd fit in.

CHARLES. Won't you give me a week's trial, madam?

LAURA. A week's trial.

CHARLES (*pressing home his advantage*). Perhaps you would like to see my references. (*He hands her some sheets of paper.*)

LAURA (*looking at the first one*). "Charles is honest, sober, industrious, a veritable treasure."

CHARLES. I was with Mr. Mallard for several years.

LAURA. Why did you leave?

CHARLES. Much to everybody's surprise, Mr. Mallard recently got married. His lady brought her major domo with her. Naturally, I could not remain in an inferior position, so I gave in my notice.

LAURA (*not seeing at all really*). I see.

CHARLES. Shall I get him on the telephone for you, madam?

LAURA. I really don't think there's any point—you see I honestly think . . .

CHARLES. I happen to know Mr. Mallard is at home this afternoon.

LAURA. Well—

CHARLES. Thank you, madam.

(*He crosses to the telephone, skilfully disentangles the twisted cord and dials.*)

LAURA. I haven't yet said that I . . .

CHARLES (*at telephone*). Hello. Mr. Mallard? This is Charles, sir. The Bureau have sent me after another position and Mrs. Pemberton, the lady of the house, would like to take up my references. (*To* LAURA.) Madam?

LAURA (*taking the receiver from* CHARLES). Good afternoon. Yes. . . . Yes, about Charles. . . . Oh. . . . Oh. . . . Is he? (*The fervent voice of* MR. MALLARD *can just be heard.*) Really? Oh. . . . And he can cook, too? Oh. . . . Yes, I'm sure you are. . . . Oh. . . . (*She is positively wilting under* MALLARD'S *enthusiasm.*) Oh. . . . Yes . . . yes. . . . Yes, I hope so . . . thank you. . . . Good-bye. (*She hangs up and turns to* CHARLES.) According to Mr. Mallard you're a cross between Jeeves and the Archangel Gabriel!

CHARLES (*with becoming modesty*). One does one's best, madam.

LAURA. Well, I suppose that settles it.

CHARLES. Thank you, madam.

(LAURA *has become entangled in the cord. He reacts and disentangles her.*)

LAURA. You'd better look at the flat first to see just what you're taking on.

CHARLES. Very good, madam.

LAURA (*opening the kitchen door*). My mother-in-law says this kitchen looks like the morning after Mafeking.

CHARLES. If I may say so, I think she has something there.

LAURA. When d'you think you'll be able to start?

CHARLES. At once, madam.

LAURA. You mean tomorrow?

CHARLES. I mean tonight, madam. Excuse me.

(*He goes to the front door, opens it and brings in a neat, anonymous-looking suitcase.*)

LAURA. Well!

CHARLES. Will you kindly let me know which is to be my room, madam?

LAURA. It's the one at the end of the passage. I'll show you.

CHARLES. Please don't trouble.

(*He starts up the stairs, carrying the suitcase. The telephone rings and* LAURA *answers it.*)

LAURA (*at telephone*). Hello? Oh, hello, Edward. . . . Yes, we're all well. . . . I see in *The Times* that you dug up something jolly exciting. . . . I'm sure it was. Where are you speaking from —Cambridge? Next week . . . yes, do. Come to tea a week today—Thursday. Yes, it's my half-day. Yes, a theatre would be heavenly. We'll decide when I see you. My domestic situation, well, actually . . .

(CHARLES *comes down the stairs. He has taken off his jacket and wears a black apron. He goes to the table and, picking up the tray, moves towards the kitchen.*)

Well, actually I have . . . yes. I'll tell you next week. No. I'm not being mysterious. Yes . . . yes. Good-bye. (*She hangs up. To* CHARLES.) That was very quick.

CHARLES. I can do it in ten seconds flat—I mean, the General was a great one for speed, madam.

LAURA. I'll come and show you where the cleaning stuff is kept.

CHARLES. Thank you, madam.

(*They move towards the kitchen, then the telephone rings and* LAURA *goes over to answer it, as* CHARLES *goes on into the kitchen.*)

LAURA (*at telephone*). Hello? Oh, Miss Benson. Oh, you have? Well, I'm afraid it's too late. I think I'm suited.

CURTAIN

SCENE 2

The same a week later and once again four o'clock in the afternoon.

As the curtain rises the telephone is heard ringing. CHARLES, *wearing a white jacket, comes out of the kitchen and crosses to answer it.*

CHARLES (*at telephone*).   Hello?   Yes. . . . Yes, Mrs. Pemberton's
houseman speaking. Oh, it's you, Cosmo. Listen, for the love
of Pete don't start ringing up. Yes, they're all out as a matter of
fact, but they might not be. Yes, I'm doing pretty well. Yes, she's
sweet. The daughters? I've only seen the little one. How's darling
Angela? Give her my love.
          (*The front door bell is heard ringing.*) ·
There's the front door bell. Listen, don't ring up if you can help
it, or if you must, use another name. . . . Oh, what the hell does
it matter *what* name! Bye.
          (*He hangs up, crosses to the door and opens it.* EDWARD
     LLEWELLYN, *a famous Welsh archaeologist, stands on the threshold.*
     EDWARD *is in his fifties. He is that very pleasant thing to be, a success-
     ful university don with private means. He has been devoted to* LAURA
     *for years but, as she surmised, even more devoted to his comforts. He has
     appeared on television and writes detective stories under the pseudonym of
     Glen Dower. He stares at* CHARLES *in astonishment.*)
EDWARD.   Good God!
CHARLES.   Yes, sir—shall I take your coat, sir?
EDWARD.   What is all this? You Mrs. Pemberton's butler?
CHARLES.   No, sir—general factotum. Your coat, sir. (*He takes it
     from the stupefied* EDWARD.) Madam won't be long, sir. She had
     to go down to the shop to see about some chairs which she could
     only have delivered this afternoon.
          (*He moves off with the coat.* EDWARD *looks about the room in
     some amazement—it is now remarkably neat and tidy—a place for
     everything and everything in its place.*)
EDWARD.   Been here long?
CHARLES.   A week today, sir. Would you care for a drink, sir, or will
     you wait for tea?
EDWARD.   I'll wait for tea, thank you.
CHARLES.   Thank *you*, sir.
          (*Footsteps are heard, and the front door opens and* LAURA *comes
     in.*)
LAURA.   Edward, I'm sorry I was out!
EDWARD.   That's all right, my dear. Anyway, I was early. Fenner of
     Corpus gave me a lift up and Jehu has nothing on him.
LAURA.   We'll have tea now, Charles.
CHARLES.   Very good, madam.
          (*He withdraws into the kitchen.*)

EDWARD. Who on earth is that?

LAURA. That's Charles.

EDWARD. Charles? Where d'you get him?

LAURA. From an agency. He's simply splendid. Don't you think the flat looks different?

EDWARD. Well, I must say I do.

LAURA. Almost as if your wonderful Mrs. Sandham had been at it?

EDWARD. I'm very worried about Mrs. Sandham—I'll tell you later. But first of all we ought to decide what we want to see tonight. Fenner says there's a very interesting play by that new Finnish author at the Royal Court.

LAURA. Edward, darling, I don't quite honestly think it's me—do you?

EDWARD. You always persist in underrating your intelligence, Laura.
    (CHARLES *enters with a tea trolley upon which is laid an exquisite tea.*)

LAURA. You know perfectly well that what I like in the theatre is a nice cosy play set in a nice cosy flat somewhere near Harrods and a cast simply riddled with knights and dames.
    (*During the next part of the dialogue,* CHARLES *hands tea etc. to* EDWARD *and* LAURA.)

EDWARD. Very well, my dear. What is there that answers to all those requirements?

LAURA. Goodness knows.

CHARLES. If I may be permitted to offer a suggestion, madam, there is "Mighty like a rose" at the Beaumont. It's the story of a duchess in distress. It's by the author of all those plays about debutantes in distress and extremely hilarious.

EDWARD. You seen it?

CHARLES. Yes, sir. I took my Aunt Edna. We both enjoyed it very much.
    (*Having organized the tea,* CHARLES *goes back into the kitchen and shuts the door.*)

EDWARD. Laura, did you get proper references with that man?

LAURA. Of course, Edward, he's an absolute treasure. There's nothing he can't do. We've never been so comfortable in our lives—even with Nannie.

EDWARD. I could swear I'd seen him before.

LAURA. Did you know General Sir Archibald Ismay-Rotherhithe? He was with him for years.

EDWARD. Who says so?

LAURA. He says so.

EDWARD. Laura, I must speak to you seriously.

LAURA. Oh no—please, please don't. I can't bear it when people speak to me seriously—tell me about your delicious burial urn instead, and what's all this about Mrs. Sandham?

EDWARD (*tragically*). Mrs. Sandham is thinking about getting married again.

LAURA. Oh dear—not to someone she's met on a bus from Chelsea?

EDWARD. No, to someone she met on an outing to Broadstairs.

LAURA. But, if she's only *thinking* of it, Edward . . .

EDWARD (*darkly*). She's been very strange lately. I had Fenner, Parks of Trinity and old Roland Burris to dinner the other night and the Crème Brûlée was tepid and the Mouton Rothschild iced.

LAURA. Edward, how awful!

EDWARD (*bravely*). One rises above such things, my dear, but when one has some sort of reputation as a host. . . . However, let's talk of other things. How is Caroline?

LAURA. I don't know. She went to a party a week ago today and hasn't come back.

EDWARD. Laura!

LAURA. Oh, it's perfectly all right. She's staying with a dreary girl-friend called Cassandra Thomas somewhere in Chelsea and rings up —well, practically every day.

EDWARD. What those girls of yours need is a firm hand. (*He rises.*) Well, my dear, I must be off. I'm having a drink with Brockway at the Athenaeum. He's got a most interesting theory about early British burials. We're thinking of doing a T.V. series about it. I'll get seats for the play and then we'll go on to supper somewhere. What about the Savoy?

LAURA. Why not come to supper here?

EDWARD (*hastily*). I wouldn't dream of giving you the trouble.

LAURA. Oh, it's not *me* that would have the trouble. (*She goes to the kitchen door and opens it.*) Charles, can you come here for a moment?

(CHARLES *enters from the kitchen.*)

CHARLES. Yes, madam.

LAURA. I've asked Mr. Llewellyn to have supper here after the theatre. Is that all right?

CHARLES. Perfectly, madam. May I suggest a little clear soup, a chicken fricassée, salad and perhaps a water ice. And to drink, a bottle of Asconia sixty-four.

LAURA (*to* EDWARD). Well?

EDWARD (*staggered*). Asconia sixty-four?

CHARLES. I took the liberty of suggesting that madam ordered a dozen bottles.

EDWARD. You did very well.

CHARLES. Thank you, sir. (*To* LAURA.) May I clear, madam?

LAURA. Thank you. (*To* EDWARD, *with the air of one making conversation.*) How's Cambridge?

EDWARD. Visually delightful—intellectually the usual vacuum. (*He pauses, and then turns to* CHARLES.) I never thought it was safe to travel Asconia?

CHARLES. This consignment came by air, sir.

(*He goes out pushing the trolley.*)

EDWARD. My dear Laura, that's a very remarkable man.

LAURA (*happily*). Isn't he?

EDWARD. Most remarkable.

LAURA. I keep pinching myself to see if it's really true or not.

EDWARD. But why should a man like that do a job like this?

LAURA. He likes it. You know, he absolutely bull-dozed me into taking him.

EDWARD. I'm *sure* I've seen him before somewhere.

LAURA. He *learns* so quickly. I mean, he was a bit hazy about detergents and things like that at first.

EDWARD. Hazy about detergents?

LAURA. Yes, and about washing out tea cloths and using the vacuum cleaner, but I only had to show him once and he had it perfectly.

EDWARD. He's certainly not hazy about food and drink.

LAURA. You know, he even gets Julia to help with the washing up?

EDWARD. Then the man's a genius—there's no more to be said. (*He rises.*) I'll call for you about quarter to seven, my dear. (*He kisses her hand and moves to the door.*) Oh, my coat—Charles took it.

LAURA (*at kitchen door*). Charles, Mr. Llewellyn's coat.

(CHARLES *emerges from the kitchen with the coat over his arm and · helps* EDWARD *into it.*)

EDWARD. Er, thank you. Well, good-bye, Laura—quarter to seven, and mind you're ready.

(*He goes out and* CHARLES *closes the door behind him.*)

LAURA. Mr. Llewellyn was very impressed by your knowledge of food and wine, Charles.

CHARLES. I'm glad, madam. Mr. Llewellyn, as I well know, is a connoisseur of such things.

LAURA. You've seen him on television, I expect.

CHARLES. I've also read several of his detective novels. I particularly enjoyed "The Don it was that died", the one in which the Master of Trinity is murdered by a colonial bishop disguised as a barrow boy.

LAURA. Why do all university dons write murder stories?

CHARLES. It's an outlet for their repressed desires towards the undergraduates, madam.

LAURA. You mean, they want to murder all those nice simple boys!

CHARLES. Boys are rarely nice, madam, and never simple.

LAURA. Who said that? I mean, it's a quotation, isn't it?

CHARLES. Not quite, madam.

LAURA. You've had a good education, Charles?

CHARLES. Until my father died, madam, I had the best of everything.

LAURA. When did he die?

CHARLES. Nineteen sixty-six.

LAURA. Nineteen sixty-six?—but surely . . .

CHARLES. I mean, *forty-six*. Nineteen sixty-six was the year my godfather died. . . . Will Miss Julia be in for tea, madam?

LAURA. Yes.

(She crosses towards the staircase.)

And ask her not to disturb me—I have some business letters I simply must write.

CHARLES. Very good, madam.

(LAURA *goes upstairs.* CHARLES *takes the tray into the kitchen and then comes back and starts to tidy up the room. He treats it as if it were a stage set and fiddles with the lights, muttering something about "needing more amber". Finally, he has it just as he wants it and starts to rearrange the china on the mantel-shelf, singing as he does so.*

(Singing.) "Oh mistress mine, where are you roaming?

Oh stay and hear your true love's coming

That can sing both high and low.

(JULIE *appears in the doorway unseen by* CHARLES. *She is wearing a dark coat over a plain dress.)*

Trip no further, pretty sweeting,

Journey's end in lovers' meeting,

Every wise man's son doth know."

JULIA (*singing*). "What is love? 'tis not hereafter."

(CHARLES *swings round.*)

"Present mirth hath present laughter."

CHARLES (*joining in*). "What's to come is still unsure."

BOTH (*singing*). "In delay there lies no plenty,
Then come kiss me, sweet and twenty,
Youth's a stuff will not endure."

(*They both burst out laughing.*)

JULIA. I say, you do sing jolly well.

CHARLES. So do you, Miss Julia.

JULIA. Fancy you knowing "Twelfth Night"! I mean— (*She pauses, embarrassed.*)

CHARLES. We did it at school.

JULIA. So did we—we acted it, too. I was Viola.

CHARLES. You'd be a good Viola.

JULIA (*thrilled*). Oh, do you think so? Have you ever acted in it? ·

CHARLES. Er—yes.,

JULIA. At school?

CHARLES (*thankfully*). At school.

JULIA. Did you ever see John Neville as Malvolio?

CHARLES. Yes.

JULIA. Wasn't he just the greatest? I mean he was the most, wasn't he?

CHARLES. Indeed he was.

JULIA. What did you play when you did it at school?

CHARLES. Orsino.

JULIA. I'm not awfully fond of Orsino, are you? I mean, I think he
was rather wet, you know, kind of sloppy.

CHARLES. Personally I've always thought he was just plain stupid.
That's no way to get a woman, just sitting about and mooning, is it?

JULIA. He'd have been miserable with Olivia, anyway. She wasn't his
type at all.

CHARLES. "Thou dost speak masterly;
My life upon't, young as thou art, thine eye
Hath stay'd upon some favour that it loves.
Hath it not, boy?"

JULIA. "A little, by your favour."

CHARLES. "What kind of woman is't?"

JULIA. "Of your complexion."

CHARLES. "She is not worth thee then. What years, i' faith?"

JULIA. "About your years, my lord."
CHARLES. "Too old, by heaven: Let still the woman take
An elder than herself, so wears she to him,
So sways she level in her husband's heart,
For boy . . ." (*He stops, realizing he is playing the scene for all it's worth.*)
JULIA. Go on! I say, you're jolly good!
CHARLES. I don't remember any more. I must get your tea, Miss Julia.
JULIA. I've had tea, or rather I've had a pound and a half of Cadbury's Dairy Milk. It was geography, you see.
CHARLES. I don't, I'm afraid.
JULIA. Well, I've got to take it for my G.C.E. and it's so utterly dreary that one must do something. I mean, what use would it be to me as an actress to know about the annual rainfall in Nicaragua?
CHARLES. You're going to be an actress?
JULIA. Oh yes. I've got another two years at school, worse luck, and then I'm going to the R.A.D.A. Oh dear, I do wish one could grow up faster. I'm terrified to think that when I'm good enough to act with John Neville he'll be past it!
CHARLES (*quickly*). John Neville's only in his forties!
JULIA. Yes, but I'm not quite fifteen.
CHARLES. When did you first decide you wanted to go on the stage?
JULIA. When I was eight. Mummy took us to "The Dream" at the Old Vic. You see, I'd no idea what the real theatre was like. I'd only seen films and T.V.
CHARLES. You poor lost generation!
JULIA. And when the orchestra started to tune up I got all gooseflesh, and then when the curtain went up—you know that funny little noise it makes that isn't a noise at all really?
CHARLES. Yes, I know.
JULIA. Well, after a few minutes—it was terribly funny—it was as if the people on the stage were the real people and not the audience, and as if the trees on the backcloth were much more real than, say, the trees you can see from that window and. . . . I'm afraid I'm not explaining it very well.
CHARLES. You're explaining it very well indeed, and now, Cadbury's Dairy Milk or not, I'm going to get you your tea, because *I* need a cup even if you don't.
JULIA. Can I help?

CHARLES. You mean, can you hinder? No, thanks. (*He goes into the kitchen—calling.*) We've got one of those whistling kettles. It wails just like our family banshee.

JULIA (*calling*). Whose family banshee?

CHARLES (*calling*). Mine.

JULIA (*calling*). Do families have banshees?

CHARLES (*calling*). All Irish families do.

JULIA (*calling*). But you're not Irish.

CHARLES (*reappearing with tray*). My grandmother came from Tipperary and she travelled her banshee everywhere. She even took it to Claridges. Have a sandwich.

JULIA (*giggling and eating*). What does a banshee look like?

CHARLES. This one looked exactly like Alfred, Lord Tennyson, so of course that was all right with Claridges.

  (*The kettle starts to scream and* CHARLES *runs into the kitchen.*)

JULIA (*calling*). Charles!

CHARLES (*calling*). Wait a moment.

  (JULIA *sits humming "O Mistress Mine" to herself.* CHARLES *reappears with the tea.*)

JULIA. You know, Charles, I only just noticed it when you were talking about banshees, but you look a tiny bit like—him.

CHARLES. Like—er—John Neville?

JULIA. Yes, not *really*, of course, but, well, there's something . . .

CHARLES. I'm flattered. Milk, Miss Julia?

JULIA. Yes, please. Charles?

CHARLES. Yes, Miss Julia. Sugar?

JULIA. Please, three lumps, no, four. Charles, do you like it here?

CHARLES. Very much, Miss Julia.

JULIA. But why *are* you here? I mean, you're so clever and so—and well, this isn't really much of a job, is it?

CHARLES. It suits me, Miss Julia.

JULIA. I know, but that's not the point. I mean—oh dear, Mummy said she'd fine me a penny every time I said "I mean" and "you know" and give the money to Dr. Barnardo's Homes.

CHARLES. They'll be able to build several new ones with the proceeds.

JULIA. Don't be beastly. I mean, what I was trying to say was surely you could get a much better one? Why, you could even go on the stage! You know you really did that Orsino bit as well as my friend, George Dennis, did and he's had two terms at L.A.M.D.A. Charles,

listen, why don't you try for a scholarship at a Drama School?
Why—

CHARLES (*interrupting*). Thank you, Miss Julia, but I'm quite happy
where I am.

JULIA. But, Charles, have you no spirit? Don't you care?

CHARLES. Of course I care, Miss Julia, but—

JULIA. But what?

> (CHARLES *realizes he will have to head her off the subject, and the*
> *instinctive actor in him, plus the vague memory of a part once played in*
> *"Rep", comes to his aid.*)

CHARLES (*significantly*). It's my weakness, Miss Julia.

JULIA. Your weakness?

CHARLES. It's the little things. I can't resist the little things.

JULIA. Little things?

CHARLES (*acting like mad*). You ask yourself why I am content to stay
here in a menial capacity? Why I am not out in the world as a
captain of industry, a leader of commerce? It's wrist-watches,
Miss Julia. I once found I had over twenty wrist-watches in my
bureau drawer.

JULIA. Wrist-watches?

CHARLES. And lighters, and cigarette-cases and small trinkets of all
kinds.

JULIA. You mean you'd *stolen* them?

CHARLES. Yes, Miss Julia.

JULIA. But, Charles, how awful!

CHARLES. It comes over me in spasms. For months I'll be perfectly all
right, and then—then it suddenly comes over me. (*Shuddering
realistically.*)

JULIA. But it's a *disease*, isn't it?

CHARLES. Kleptomania.

JULIA. But if it's a disease can't they cure it?

CHARLES. Not in the advanced stages.

JULIA. Is yours advanced?

CHARLES. Very advanced.

JULIA. Oh, Charles, I'm so dreadfully sorry.

CHARLES. Thank you, miss. (*He puts out hand and is about to pick up a
silver match-box, but stops.*) You see, Miss Julia, it was starting to
come over me. If you hadn't been here I'd have pocketed it. Of
course I'd have returned it, but still . . .

JULIA. Would you?

CHARLES. Oh, yes. I always return things.

JULIA. Have you always stolen. . . . I mean taken things?

CHARLES. Since I was a tot. They found a positive cache of other babies' dummies in my pram once. I'm told there was a very ugly scene in Kensington Gardens.

JULIA. So that is why you take jobs like this?

CHARLES. Yes, miss. I never last long anywhere, of course.

JULIA. But if you return things?

CHARLES. I know, Miss Julia, but most people object to having them taken in the first place.

JULIA (*making up her mind*). Charles, I'm going to help you.

CHARLES. Thank you, Miss Julia.

JULIA. First of all you must promise to let me know when you feel it coming over you.

CHARLES. Very good, miss.

JULIA. And once a week *I* will turn out your pockets, and go through your chest of drawers to see it there's anything you've forgotten to send back.

CHARLES. Er—thank you, miss.

JULIA. Don't worry, Charles. I'm sure if you try hard and with me to help you it will come over you less and less.

(CHARLES *is genuinely touched and drops the role of kleptomaniac as quickly as he has taken it up.*)

CHARLES. I hope so, Miss Julia.

JULIA. You see, it isn't as though you had a wife. You haven't, have you?

CHARLES. Not now.

JULIA. Oh dear, did she die?

CHARLES. No, she just met someone very much richer.

JULIA. How beastly of her!

CHARLES. How practical!

JULIA. Were you terribly upset?

CHARLES. At the time.

JULIA. Charles, I know I'm young, but—I mean, if I could sort of understudy . . . you see, a man really does need a woman to help him. . . . You know, like Bassanio and Portia . . . and I do like you awfully, Charles.

CHARLES (*smiling*). And I like you, Miss Julia.

JULIA. Oh, good! (*She holds out her hand.* CHARLES *takes it.* LAURA *appears on the staircase, letters in hand.*) And your secret's safe with me, you know. I'll never let on to a soul. (*She sees* LAURA's *surprised look and drops his hand.* CHARLES, *following her gaze, sees* LAURA *also.*) Oh, hello, Mummy.

CHARLES. Shall I take your letters, madam? I've just got to pop out to the delicatessen before it closes.

>   (LAURA *hands him the letters and he pushes the trolley out into the kitchen.*)

JULIA (*making conversation*). We had a simply heavenly art class today, Mummy. Angela Stone, you know the one you said looked like a punctured balloon, well she fainted dead away, so of course, there was no end of a fuss and old Gibbons just left us to draw what we liked.

>   (CHARLES *emerges from the kitchen in a coat and goes out through the front door.*)

So I drew Angela fainting, only I pretended she'd been shot and put masses of crimson lake for blood. It looked so absolutely terrifying that Moira . . .

LAURA (*interrupting*). What on earth was going on between you and Charles just now?

JULIA. Going on between me and Charles? Nothing, Mummy. Well, as I was saying, Moira said that . . .

LAURA (*interrupting*). What was all that about a secret?

JULIA (*impressively*). Mummy, Charles told me something very, very personal, and I said I wouldn't let anyone know what it was, that's all.

LAURA. But why should he tell anything "very, very personal" to a child like you?

JULIA. Mummy, I'm fourteen. When Juliet was fourteen, she was married.

>   (*She moves towards the staircase with dignity. As she passes the table she picks up the silver match-box.*)

LAURA. Juliet was a foreigner, and it was all a very long time ago. Julia, what are you doing with that match-box?

JULIA. Mummy, don't you think there are too many small things about the room? You see, I mean . . .

LAURA (*interrupting*). That'll be twopence.

JULIA. Well, don't you think it would be much nicer if it were barer?

LAURA. No, I don't.

JULIA. Have you ever thought that by leaving things like this lying about you were exposing people to temptation?

LAURA. Julia, what are you talking about?

JULIA. What would you do if . . . oh, never mind.

LAURA. Darling, is this one of your days for being misunderstood by mother?

JULIA. No, Mummy, it's only. . . . Mummy, couldn't you put away some of those china figures? Honestly the place looks horribly cluttered.

LAURA. Since when have you worried about cluttering? I looked into your room just now . . . all those filthy little glass animals on the bookcase.

JULIA (*quickly*). I'm going to give them all to Moira. I'm not going to have anything in my room that could possibly . . .

LAURA. That could possibly what?

JULIA. Oh, nothing. (*She starts to mount the staircase.*) Mummy, does Charles remind you of anyone?

LAURA. No, should he?

JULIA. Well, it's only now and again, but he's a tiny bit like John Neville, don't you think?

LAURA. Well, they're both tall.

JULIA (*starry-eyed*). Yes, that must be it, they're both tall.

(*The telephone rings.* LAURA *picks it up.*)

LAURA. Hello! Hello, Mamma-in-law. Yes, I sold it, and I got thirteen pounds, so sucks to you, darling.

(JULIA *disappears up the stairs.*)

Yes, we're all jolly well. How's Pa's gout? Oh, good. Yes, he's wonderful. You wouldn't recognize the flat but . . . well, he seems to be up to something with Julia. Oh no, not that sort of thing! No, I think she's got one of her crushes on him and he's playing up. Oh, she's being cryptic and talking about Juliet. Yes, I suppose we all did, even you? Darling, *not* an archdeacon? Well, I've always thought there was something very sexy about those gaiters. No, I'm not worried. It'll be a change from John Neville, anyway. Thank goodness I've never had anything like that with Caroline. She never looks at a man, she's so busy with her nasty little bits of celluloid. I suppose I'll have to speak to him about Julia, and tell him to slap her down or something. It's all very tiresome.

Attractive? Oh, I suppose so, tall and dark and all that. Well, come and see for yourself. No, darling, there's no fear of that as far as I'm concerned. If he were the last . . .

(*The front door opens and* CHARLES *reappears carrying some small parcels. He crosses into the kitchen.*)

Why, it's nearly six. I must go and dress. I'm going to the theatre with Edward. All right, darling, see you next week. Bye.

(*She hangs up.* CHARLES *appears with sherry on a tray. He puts it on the sideboard.*)

CHARLES. Shall I prepare some sandwiches for when Mr. Llewellyn comes, madam?

LAURA. Oh, er, yes, please, Charles.

(*He turns to go back into kitchen.*)

Charles!

CHARLES (*turning back*). Yes, madam?

LAURA (*making up her mind*). Charles, I . . .

(*Before she can say her piece about* JULIA *the front door opens and* CAROLINE *appears, looking, if possible, more farouche than usual.*)

CAROLINE. Well, Mummy. (*She stares at* CHARLES.)

LAURA. Hello, darling. (*To* CHARLES.) Thank you, Charles.

CHARLES. Thank you, madam. (*Goes into kitchen and shuts the door.*)

CAROLINE. Who on earth's that? -

LAURA. That's our new help.

CAROLINE. But it's fantastic!

LAURA. What is?

CAROLINE. But he's exactly like the man who played the First hop-picker in my film. The same look of peasant suffering and deep personal frustration. The same sort of primeval despair. You saw the film, Mummy. Don't you notice it?

LAURA (*weakly*). Well, they're both tall.

CAROLINE (*starry-eyed*). Yes, they're both tall.

She goes off towards the staircase in a dream. LAURA *pours herself out a stiff sherry and*

THE CURTAIN FALLS.

ACT TWO

It is Saturday afternoon a few days later. We notice that JULIA *has had her way, for all the small objects have been removed.*

> *There is a ring at the front door bell.* CHARLES *comes out of the kitchen, crosses to the door and opens it.* MRS. PEMBERTON *is on the threshold.* LAURA, *in a dressing gown, runs down the stairs.*

LAURA. Hello, darling.

MRS. P. (*entering*). I thought we were going to look at that tea service.

LAURA (*kissing her*). We are, only I got so filthy unpacking all the Waterford this morning that I had to have a bath. Would you like some coffee while I dress?

> (MRS. PEMBERTON *nods.*)

(*To* CHARLES.) Charles, will you bring some coffee for Mrs. Pemberton.

CHARLES. Very good, madam. (*Goes into kitchen.*)

MRS. P. So that's him!

LAURA. Yes, that's him.

MRS. P. Most impressive! How's Julia?

LAURA. You mean *who's* Julia? At the moment I think she's Desdemona to Charles' Othello. John Neville has taken quite a back stall.

MRS. P. Well, I must say your man's definitely got an air. Now, whom does he—

LAURA (*interrupting*). Remind you of?

MRS. P. Yes. I know it's—

LAURA (*interrupting again*). Your archdeacon!

MRS. P. Well, as a matter of fact it is, in an odd sort of way. You see, they're both—

> (LAURA *gives a strangled yelp.*)

Why, what is the matter?

LAURA. Nothing, darling, nothing. Well, I must go and dress. I won't be long. (*Moves to staircase.*)

MRS. P. What's happened to this room? It looks awfully bare.

LAURA. Julia has developed a complex about small objects.

MRS. P. What do you mean?

LAURA. What does *she* mean is more to the point.

MRS. P. Is Caroline back?
LAURA. Yes.
MRS. P. How is she?
LAURA. Translated.

> (*She disappears.* MRS. P. *looks after her in bewilderment.* CHARLES *emerges from the kitchen with coffee on a tray. He places it on a small table by* MRS. P.)

CHARLES. Cream and sugar, madam?
MRS. P. Thank you. (*She looks at him kindly and decides to draw him out.*)
    Well, er, Charles, have you quite settled in?
CHARLES. Yes, thank you, madam.
MRS. P. I gather that you come from some sort of ex-servicemen's
    organization?
CHARLES. Yes, madam.
MRS. P. Who runs it?
CHARLES. A Colonel Berenger, madam.
MRS. P. Berenger. . . . Berenger? I knew a Berenger once. Was he
    in the II.L.I.?
CHARLES. No, madam, he was a gunner.
MRS. P. Oh, then I don't know him. Were you a gunner?
CHARLES. No, madam. I was in the Territorial Army in Wales.
MRS. P. You're Welsh, then?
CHARLES. No, madam, but my grandmother came from Tonypandy.
MRS. P. Have you been doing this work long?

> (*She takes out her cigarette case.*)

CHARLES. Some years, madam.

> (*He sees her looking round for an ash tray and he deftly opens a drawer in the table and produces one.*)

Here you are, madam.
MRS. P. Thank you. But why are they kept in a drawer?
CHARLES. Well, madam—er—it's—

> (CAROLINE *appears on the staircase—a changed* CAROLINE. *She wears a blouse and a skirt. Her hair is neatly in place. She is properly made up and very pretty.*)

CAROLINE. Hello, Grannie!
MRS. P. (*turning and seeing her*). Good God!

> (CHARLES *thankfully escapes into the kitchen.* CAROLINE *casts a languishing look after him, then crosses and kisses* MRS. P.)

CAROLINE. D'you like my skirt?

MRS. P. Very much indeed. But why this thusness?

CAROLINE. Oh, one's personality's fluid, especially at my age, and this seems to be more me at the moment.

MRS. P. I'm profoundly relieved.

CAROLINE (*smiling*). Will you be seen in the streets with me now?

MRS. P. Indeed I will. I'll even take you out to lunch at the Ritz next time I get any dividends. But why aren't you at your studio or whatever it is?

CAROLINE. There's nothing much to do on Saturdays, so I thought I ought to stay at home and help Mummy.

MRS. P. (*staggered*). You what?

CAROLINE. She had all that glass to unpack. More coffee, Grannie?

MRS. P. Er, thank you.

CAROLINE (*pouring*). This isn't very hot. Would you like me to make you some fresh?

MRS. P. No, thank you. Are you quite well, Caroline?

CAROLINE. Yes, of course. Why?

MRS. P. Well, your appearance—and this sudden attack of domesticity.

CAROLINE. Well, I've realized that all that goes to make up domesticity —cooking, housework and the rest—are creative and therefore arts. And who are we to rate the importance of one art above another?

MRS. P. (*weakly*). Who, indeed?

CAROLINE. You must admit that Escoffier has his place as well as Eisenstein.

MRS. P. Who's Eisenstein?

CAROLINE. Did you never see "Potemkin"?

MRS. P. No, dear. What is it?

CAROLINE. Only one of the greatest films ever made. He directed it.

MRS. P. Grandpa and I saw a very good film last night. I can't remember what it was called, but it had Cary Grant and that nice, well bred Deborah Kerr in it. We enjoyed it immensely. It was so restful.

CAROLINE. Restful!

LAURA (*appearing on the staircase*). Sorry to have been so long. Now at what number in Vicarage Place does that woman live?

MRS. P. I gave the letter to you.

LAURA. Yes, I know. Now, where did I put it? You gave it to me in

the shop last week and I was wearing my brown suit, so it must
be in my brown bag. It's upstairs. I'll go and get it.
CAROLINE. I'll go, Mummy. (*She runs upstairs.* MRS. P. *and* LAURA
look at each other.)
MRS. P. What's happened to her?
LAURA. Charles.
MRS. P. What?
LAURA. He said he liked womanly women.
MRS. P. Caroline as well as Julia?
LAURA. Yes.
MRS. P. The man's a Mormon!
LAURA. Ssh!
    (CAROLINE *comes downstairs with the bag.* LAURA *rummages*
in it.)
Thank you, darling. Now, let me see. Ah, here it is. Number
ninety-seven. Why, that's just round the corner. (*To* CAROLINE.)
What are you doing this afternoon?
CAROLINE. I'm going to tidy my room.
    (MRS. P. *makes a choking sound.*)
LAURA. Grannie and I are going to see a tea service that some Mrs.
Rackham wants to sell. We won't be long.
MRS. P. (*going*). She says it's old Crown Derby but I bet it isn't. I
didn't like her voice on the telephone. It was overlaid, if you know
what I mean.
LAURA (*going*). I don't.
MRS. P. (*going*). Yes, you do. S.W. three over S.E. two.
    (*They go out, closing the door behind them.* CAROLINE *picks up*
the coffee tray but in so doing spills some coffee.)
CAROLINE. Blast! (CHARLES *re-enters from the kitchen.*) Oh, Charles,
I'm so sorry, I've spilt some coffee.
CHARLES. I'll get a cloth, miss. (*Goes into the kitchen and returns with*
cloth.)
CAROLINE. Let me do it.
CHARLES. That's all right, miss.
    (*There is a pause while* CHARLES *mops up.*)
CAROLINE. Grannie was absolutely astounded to see me in a skirt.
CHARLES. Was she, miss?
CAROLINE. You know, if we hadn't been discussing Ingrid Bergman
the other morning while we were washing up, I don't suppose I'd
have realized my essential womanliness.

CHARLES. Yes, you would, Miss Caroline. It was bound to hit you some time.

CAROLINE. Cassandra Thomas—she works in the cutting rooms with me—thinks I look horribly bourgeoise. But then I suppose I am. She got quite nasty and even said I'd end up in feature films.

CHARLES. Is that so terrible?

CAROLINE. Well, you can't *say* anything in them.

CHARLES. And what do you want to say?

CAROLINE. I'm not quite sure at the moment, but one day—goodness knows when—I will be, and that's what's so exciting.

CHARLES (*smiling, for she has suddenly become as young as* JULIA *and dropped her poses*). And you have found the right medium in which to say it?

CAROLINE. I think so. No, I'm sure about that at least. You see, the film—not the feature—that's a hybrid of the novel and the theatre —but the film *per se* is a really pure art form and . . . and . . . oh dear, I'm afraid I'm rather incoherent.

CHARLES. No, I think I understand what you mean, but I'm sorry you don't share my consuming passion.

CAROLINE. What for?

CHARLES. Westerns!

CAROLINE (*scornfully*). Westerns!

CHARLES (*dramatically*). It's evening in Dodge City. Main Street is full of people and the saloon is fuller still with rough, tough characters drinking and gambling. A stranger rides down the street, a lean, gaunt man with his lips set in a grim line. As he passes by, the people cease talking and avert their eyes. He stops outside the saloon, dismounts, hitches his horse and enters. As he walks to the bar the drinkers and gamblers fall silent and stand watching. He pulls out some money, puts it down on the bar and asks for a drink. "I ain't serving you, mister," says the barman. A shot shatters the mirror behind the barman's head and the stranger swings round, a gun miraculously appearing in each hand, and then Good-Time Gertie, her eyes blazing, steps forward and— (*He pauses.*)

CAROLINE (*breathlessly*). Go on!

CHARLES. You see? It may not be great art, Miss Caroline, but it's jolly exciting.

CAROLINE. I suppose it is, and I must admit that even Peter Hollis likes Westerns.

CHARLES. Who's he?

CAROLINE. One of our editors.

CHARLES. Obviously a sensible fellow.

CAROLINE (*trying to look up from under her lashes*). He likes me, too.

CHARLES. An even more sensible fellow. (*Starts to move off with the tray again.*)

CAROLINE (*endeavouring to be casual*). He wants me to be his mistress.

CHARLES (*swinging round*). What!

CAROLINE. Well, after all, I'm seventeen. It's awfully Victorian to be seventeen and still a virgin.

CHARLES. It is not!

CAROLINE. Cassandra Thomas says it is. She says I ought to go to bed with him because—

CHARLES (*interrupting*). Damn Cassandra Thomas. Does your mother know about this?

CAROLINE. Of course not. One doesn't tell one's parents these things.

CHARLES. Why not?

CAROLINE. Well, Mummy'd be so worried. I—I couldn't.

CHARLES. Now listen, Miss Caroline. I have three things to say to you. It's not my place to say them, but after what you've told me I'm going to. First, going to bed with anyone because some bogus little fool says you ought to is just plain messy. Second, your mother is the one person you *do* tell. And third, I'd like to have that Cassandra Thomas here and slap her bottom—hard!

CAROLINE. I think she'd like that. She's a terrific masochist.

CHARLES. And now, if you'll excuse me, Miss Caroline, I must get back to my work. (*He starts to move off once more.*)

CAROLINE. Charles.

CHARLES (*patiently*). Yes, miss.

CAROLINE. You're very helpful to me. I wish I could help you.

CHARLES. Thank you, miss.

CAROLINE. I've been thinking very seriously about you, you know.

CHARLES. Have you, miss?

CAROLINE. Oh, I know no effort is ever wasted and I know that Escoffier has his place as well as Eisenstein. I just said so to Grannie, but—

CHARLES. But what, miss?

CAROLINE. But surely you were meant for something better.

CHARLES. Thank you, Miss Caroline. I'm quite satisfied with my lot.

CAROLINE. You ought not to be.

CHARLES. But I am, miss. (*Going.*)

CAROLINE. Have you never had any ambition? I mean when—when

you were a little boy, what did you want to be when you grew up?
CHARLES. A hermit.
CAROLINE. That's very interesting psychologically. Have you ever
    been analysed? Have you ever really come to grips with your ego?
CHARLES. My ego has lasted me very nicely all these years, Miss
    Caroline and—
CAROLINE. But there must be some sort of traumatic block somewhere.
    You're an intelligent, sensitive, good-looking man. You should be
    very successful, and yet something is holding you back. It isn't as
    if you had any special weakness—
CHARLES. Weakness—
CAROLINE. Well, you don't drink or anything like that. I'm deter-
    mined to wake some ambition in you. Charles, have you no spirit?
    Don't you care?
CHARLES (*unable to resist his cue and accepting it as a means of escape*). But
    I do, Miss Caroline.
CAROLINE. You do care?
CHARLES. No, drink. I can't resist taking little nips.
CAROLINE. Little nips?
CHARLES. Yes, miss. Whisky preferably.
CAROLINE. Charles!
CHARLES (*entering into the spirit of the role*). It's in the family, miss.
    Why, when my Uncle William cut his throat after an unfortunate
    week at Monte Carlo they say he bled vintage port. And my
    cousin, Arthur—
CAROLINE. It's not a joking matter.
CHARLES. No, miss.
CAROLINE. I've never seen you drunk.
CHARLES. Oh, I can stay off the stuff for weeks on end and then
    suddenly I feel it coming over me. (*Looks at the drink tray on the
    sideboard.*) If you weren't here, Miss Caroline I—yes, I'm afraid it
    might come over me now.
CAROLINE. Have you seen a doctor?
CHARLES. Several doctors.
CAROLINE. Weren't they any use?
CHARLES. One of them suggested that every time I felt like taking a
    little nip I ate an apple instead.
CAROLINE. Did that help?
CHARLES. Miss Caroline, one cannot eat thirty-six apples before lunch!
CAROLINE. Charles, this is terrible!

CHARLES. I know, miss.

CAROLINE. Did any of them suggest your being analysed? You know, I can't help thinking—

CHARLES. They said it would be the worst thing possible for me. They said the person who should have been analysed was the ancestor who started it all. "Ten-bottle" Timothy he was called.

CAROLINE. Charles, even if analysis is no good, I'm sure I can help you.

CHARLES. Thank you, miss.

CAROLINE. Whenever you feel it coming over you, you must let me know at once and I'll hide away all the drink—in fact I think I'd better hide it away anyhow.

CHARLES. No, Miss Caroline—

CAROLINE (*interrupting*). I am not going to have you exposed to temptation!

(*She crosses to the drinks tray and picks up a bottle of sherry in one hand and a bottle of whisky in the other.*)

CHARLES. Miss Caroline, you can't do that!

(*The telephone starts to ring.*)

CAROLINE. Answer it, will you, Charles?

(*She runs upstairs with the bottles, and* CHARLES, *muttering, crosses to the telephone.*)

CHARLES (*at telephone*). Yes? Yes, sir. Very good, sir. (*Hangs up.* Miss Caroline! (*Calling.*)

(*The door opens and* LAURA *and* MRS. P. *enter.*)

Mr. Llewellyn just rang, madam, and said he would be looking in about six.

LAURA. Thank you, Charles.

(CHARLES *goes into the kitchen and shuts the door.*)

MRS. P. Well, I was right, wasn't I? As bogus as her voice. Crown Derby indeed! Cheap modern rubbish!

LAURA. I think we ought to buy it, though.

(CAROLINE *descends the stairs.*)

MRS. P. Are you mad?

LAURA. You remember she said she'd throw in all the stuff in that corner cupboard as well?

MRS. P. More rubbish!

LAURA. Not all of it. You didn't look properly.

MRS. P. No need to. I saw some horrible Beleek cups, and that was enough for me.

LAURA. Behind the Beleek was a Nantgarw coffee set.

MRS. P. (*collapsing into chair*). No!

CAROLINE. What's Nantgarw?

LAURA. It's a little place in South Wales that turned out the most exquisite china for a short period during the last century. It's now very rare and very valuable.

MRS. P. You're certain it's Nantgarw?

LAURA. Absolutely. (*Opens handbag and takes out small cup.*) I thought you'd want to check it.

MRS. P. Laura!

CAROLINE. Mummy!

LAURA. I'll put it back tomorrow when I go round to say we've decided to buy the phony Crown Derby.

MRS. P. Give it to me. (*Taking the cup.*) Yes, it's Nantgarw all right. Oh, you pretty thing! I know just the home for you in Boston, Massachusetts, with some very, very lovely people who have a lot of very, very lovely money. Laura Pemberton, you never cease to surprise me. It's I who need a keeper, not you. Now can I have a strong drink, please, before I go for my train?

LAURA. Caroline, give Grannie a whisky. Oh, I'll have one, too.

(CAROLINE *stands irresolutely and then moves towards the staircase.*)

Darling, did you hear what I said?

CAROLINE. Yes, Mummy. I'm just going to get it.

LAURA. But it's— (*She sees it is not on the table and looks at* CAROLINE *in surprise.*)

CAROLINE. I took it up to my room.

LAURA. You what?

CAROLINE. Do you think it morally right to have drinks about? It could be a terrible temptation.

LAURA. To whom?

MRS. P. Have you joined the Band of Hope or something?

CAROLINE. I'll bring it down if you insist, but I really think that out of common humanity it should be kept under lock and key. (*She goes upstairs with dignity.*)

MRS. P. Well!

LAURA. I think I recognize Charles' fine Italian hand . . .

MRS. P. Does he think Caroline is a potential dipso?

LAURA. She hates drink. Now Julia adores a glass of sherry, but Caroline—

Mrs. P. Where is Julia, by the way?
Laura. Having tea with her friend, Susan Billings.
Mrs. P. Laura, if both the girls—
Laura. Ssh!

> (Caroline *comes downstairs with a bottle of whisky. She is wearing a coat.*)

Caroline. Here you are, Mummy, and please lock it up when you've had your drinks. Good-bye, Grannie.
Mrs. P. Good-bye, Caroline.
Laura (*to* Caroline). Where are you going, darling?
Caroline. Into the park. I want to think.

> (*She goes out.* Laura *lifts her eyes to heaven and pours out two drinks.*)

Laura. Really, aren't children the end!
Mrs. P. Thank the Lord I only had one girl: the rest were boys.
Laura. Are they easier?
Mrs. P. Much. I don't know why, but they are. Laura, you really must marry Edward.
Laura. Because of his firm hand?
Mrs. P. Yes. You need a man about the house.
Laura. I've got one. That seems to be the trouble.
Mrs. P. Edward wouldn't stand for any of that nonsense from the girls.
Laura. Do you think they'd take any notice of him?
Mrs. P. Of course.
Laura. I don't. Caroline doesn't consider he's "forward thinking" and Julia says he's got no "message".
Mrs. P. Really! I'd like another drink, please.
Laura. Me, too. (*She pours out two large ones.*)
Mrs. P. Laura—those are doubles!
Laura. I don't care. I've got to acquire some Dutch courage somehow.
Mrs. P. What for? Do be careful—you know what a shocking head you have.
Laura. I've got to have a heart to heart with Charles.
Mrs. P. About the girls?
Laura. About himself. I've come to the conclusion that he's as bogus as that Crown Derby. (*She takes a gulp of whisky.*) Horrible taste, isn't it? (*She takes another gulp.*) Filthy.

MRS. P. What d'you mean, Laura?

LAURA. My feminine intuition says that he isn't what he seems.

MRS. P. Do you think he's a criminal?

LAURA. Could be.

MRS. P. Rubbish!

LAURA. I was reading somewhere that criminal types have no lobes to their ears. I must have a good look at his. Don't shoot until you see the lobes of their ears! (*She giggles.*) Would you like another drink before I "lock it away"?

MRS. P. No, thank you. At this rate there'll be nothing left to lock away.

LAURA. Have you ever been drunk? Not high, but really roaring drunk?

MRS. P. Never, I'm glad to say.

LAURA (*giggling*). I have, once. When George and I went to Paris. It was wonderful. I think I'd like to try it again.

MRS. P. Well, you can't try it now. Edward's coming at six.

LAURA. All the more reason.

(*She knocks back her drink and pours herself another. By now she is just a trifle high.*)

MRS. P. Laura!

LAURA. Oh dear, do I really have to marry Edward?

MRS. P. Well, I think it would be—

LAURA (*interrupting*). The best thing possible for the girls? What about me? Would you think Edward was any good in bed?

MRS. P. I've no idea, but—

LAURA (*interrupting*). Nor have I. Wouldn't it be awful if he looked on me as a Grecian urn, a "still unravished bride of quietness"?

MRS. P. Laura, you're tight!

LAURA. I always swore I'd never marry a man who didn't make me knock at the knees. I've always wanted to knock at the knees and I never have. I adored darling George, but my knees were as steady as rock cakes when he was around.

MRS. P. Laura, I must go or I'll miss my train. Go and lie down till Edward comes, there's a good girl.

LAURA. Did you ever knock at the knees?

MRS. P. No.

LAURA. Not even when you saw the archdeacon?

MRS. P. Certainly not!

LAURA. Then you're undersexed, just like me.

MRS. P. Laura dear, do go and lie down. I *must* fly. Promise me you'll lie down. Get Charles to make you some black coffee.

LAURA. He might put some arsenic in it.

MRS. P. Rubbish!

LAURA. Charles is very, very fishy indeed, very fishy, very.

MRS. P. Rubbish!

LAURA. Darling, why don't you say "Fiddlesticks" now and again for a change? It would suit you. "Fiddlesticks!" Try it.

TOGETHER. "Fiddlesticks!"

(MRS. P. *goes out*.)

LAURA (*after a moment's pause and drawing a deep breath, calls*). Charles!

CHARLES (*entering from kitchen*). Yes, madam?

LAURA. Charles, I think it's time you and I had a heart to heart. Is there any whisky left?

CHARLES (*looking*). A little, madam.

LAURA. Then give yourself a drink and come and sit down.

CHARLES. But, madam—

LAURA. Please do as I say.

CHARLES. Very good, madam. (*He pours out a drink and crosses to her*.)

LAURA. Sit down.

CHARLES (*sitting*). Yes, madam.

LAURA. Charles, I've come to the conclusion that you're just one great big phoney!

CHARLES. Madam!

LAURA. I don't believe you've been doing this for years. I don't believe in General Sir Whosit Whatishisname Thingummy. Why is a man like you who is—well, it's almost a dirty word nowadays— but who is, let's face it, a gentleman, doing work like this. Are you some sort of crook?

CHARLES. No, madam.

(*She leans forward and peers at his ears*.)

LAURA. Well, you've got lobes all right.

CHARLES. I beg your pardon, madam?

LAURA. Well, lobes or not, what kind of nonsense have you been up to with my daughters? Now come clean, Charles.

CHARLES. Well, madam—

LAURA. While you think up a really good story, I'll have another drink.

CHARLES. I'm afraid there's no more whisky. There's some black coffee on the stove, madam. I'll get it. (*Rises and goes to kitchen*.)

LAURA (*to her empty glass*). See what you've done? You've made me tight, high, tiddley, stinking, well away, half cut, pie-eyed, shot away, one over the eight, stotious, boozed—blotto—that's a big favourite—blotto—what a lot of words for one foolish thing!
> (CHARLES *re-enters with the coffee, hands her a cup and she drinks it.*)
Ugh!
> (CHARLES *hands her a bottle of aspirin.*)
You've got it taped, haven't you?

CHARLES. Will that be all, madam?

LAURA. Not on your life! Sit down. (*He sits.*) Where were we?

CHARLES. You were asking me to think up a really good story, madam.

LAURA. And have you?

CHARLES. I suppose I'd better tell the truth.

LAURA. Why not? It'd be a change. (*She takes another gulp of coffee.*)

CHARLES. I'm not a crook. I'm an out-of-work actor.

LAURA. An actor?

CHARLES. Shall I tell you the story of my life, madam?

LAURA. Again, why not?

CHARLES. Some years ago, I was a promising young juvenile, not quite there, but on the way there. Then I was involved in a nasty car crash, that was two years in and out of hospital, and when they said I was cured, they were wrong. I wasn't. The bones hadn't set properly, or something. That meant back to hospital, and bang went another two years. So by this time I was no longer a juvenile and I found it difficult to get work. I was either too young or too old. Finally I did get a part, not a particularly good one, on a long tour of South Africa and Australia. When I came back, I found that I'd been forgotten for the second time. I did a bit of filming, the odd T.V. commercial, but it barely paid the rent. So one day my friend Cosmo Mallard told me about Colonel Berenger, who runs Service for Ladies. My father knew him, so I went to see him. He'd a lot of resting actors on his books, he said. You see actors are not trained for anything except acting, and there's nothing doing for untrained men today. While I was in the Colonel's office you rang up—and here I am.
> (*There is a pause. The room is getting dark but the sky outside the window is a brilliant pink and is reflected on their faces. The black coffee and* CHARLES' *story have had their effect on* LAURA.)

LAURA. Oh Charles, how filthy for you. I am most terribly sorry.
CHARLES. Thank you, madam.
LAURA. Can't you drop the madam?
CHARLES. I must remain in character, madam.
LAURA. But Charles, things can't be as bad as all that in the entertainment business. Why, look at I.T.V.—I mean don't look at it if you can help it—but there it is.
CHARLES. An occasional small part on television doesn't pay the rent.
LAURA. Charles, may I ask you something?
CHARLES. Of course, madam.
LAURA. Are you a good actor?
CHARLES. I was. I think nowadays I'm probably terrible. One loses confidence, you know.
LAURA. What did you play last?
CHARLES. An amateur performance of a dipsomaniac for Miss Caroline's benefit.
LAURA. What *do* you mean?
CHARLES. Well, madam, both Miss Julia and Miss Caroline have been very kindly taking an interest in me and trying to rouse my ambitions. Miss Julia wanted me to go on the stage, and Miss Caroline was very anxious for me to "express myself" in some way. They are both very determined young women. I had to protect myself.
LAURA. Well?
CHARLES. Miss Julia said to me—
LAURA. For the love of Mike say "Julia". You're not playing Crichton now. You told me all, remember?
CHARLES. Julia said, "But, Charles, don't you care?" It was a cue. I once had it years ago in some absurd piece I played in in Melbourne about a kleptomaniac. I couldn't resist it—besides I thought it would stop her trying to spur me on to be an actor.
LAURA. Did it?
CHARLES. She's a dear child and she decided to help me to fight my failing instead.
LAURA. I see. That accounts for her hiding away anything pocketable.
CHARLES. Yes. I said an uncontrollable weakness for little things came over me every now and again.
LAURA. But what about Caroline? Why did you switch from kleptomania to *drink?*
CHARLES. I can't think.
LAURA. Well, let's hope the girls don't compare notes, or you're for it.

CHARLES. I'm for it anyway.

LAURA. What d'you mean?

CHARLES. I can't stay on now.

LAURA. Charles!

CHARLES. You know I can't.

LAURA. Are you going back to the stage?

CHARLES. There's nothing on the stage for me to go back to.

LAURA. Then why can't you stay on? Don't you like us?

CHARLES. Very much.

LAURA. Well then!

CHARLES. It wouldn't work.

LAURA. I don't see why not.

CHARLES. You do, really.

LAURA. Oh dear, why did I have to get tight and ask you those questions? I wish you'd headed me off with some tall story as you did the girls.

CHARLES. So do I. But somehow I couldn't. I've never liked lying to you.

LAURA. Haven't you?

CHARLES. There's something so trusting about you.

LAURA. Is there?

CHARLES. Yes. It doesn't seem fair.

LAURA. Charles—Oh, oughtn't I to call you "Mr." something? What is your name?

CHARLES. Selby.

LAURA. Charles Selby—nice.

CHARLES. I used to think it made for neon lights.

LAURA. It may still be.

CHARLES. Not unless—Well, unless somehow that break for which every actor prays happens. You need two things for success in the theatre: talent and the chance to show it. They're interdependent. One's no good without the other.

LAURA. George, my husband, said something like that once. He said that given the right opportunity talent rose to the top like scum.

CHARLES. He was right.

LAURA. He was concerned with the theatre once, only we never speak of it in the family.

CHARLES. Why ever not?

LAURA. He backed a play and lost an awful lot of money. Do you know Sir Robert Ferrars?

CHARLES. I've met him. He was in Melbourne when I was there. He saw one of our matinées and came round afterwards. I must say he was very nice about my performance.

LAURA. Well, he was at Oxford with George and he found this play. "Tell Me Tomorrow" it was called. He wasn't well known or anything in those days but he was mad about the piece and so was George. It was a really terrible flop. Oh dear, if only we had that money now, things would be much easier.

CHARLES. Would they?

LAURA. I don't long for it any more—by now I've got over the indignity of not having a mink coat—but I do long for it for the girls.

CHARLES. It seems to me they have everything they want.

LAURA. Yes, but not everything I want for them.

CHARLES. Don't worry, they'll be all right. They're nice girls and that's what matters.

LAURA. I wish I knew them better. You've only been with us a very short time, yet you probably know more about them than I do.

CHARLES. It's often much easier to talk to a stranger.

LAURA. And to a man. They'd have talked to George.

CHARLES. How long—I mean— (*Hesitates.*)

LAURA. How long ago did he die? Ten years. It was awfully sudden. He was ill only a few days. Poor George, he did so adore being alive.

CHARLES. I'm so sorry.

LAURA. It doesn't hurt any more, of course, but at the time. . . . It wasn't as though I was wildly in love with him either, but he'd always been there. I'd known him all my life. I felt safe with him. Goodness! Here I am, pouring out everything to you just as if I were one of my daughters!

CHARLES. I'm very honoured.

LAURA. Are you married?

CHARLES. My wife ran away ten years ago with a rich Australian sheep farmer.

LAURA. Were you in love with her?

CHARLES. No, I was obsessed by her. I was mad about her, and then quite suddenly I realized that we had absolutely nothing in common and that I was profoundly bored. Of course when she left me my pride was badly hurt—but only my pride.

LAURA. Pride can be jolly painful.

CHARLES. He was very rich but when you saw him with his sheep you recognized him by the fact that he was the one that wore a hat.

LAURA. You're a bitch, aren't you?

CHARLES. Well, I—

LAURA. Men are far more bitchy than women really. You should hear Edward Llewellyn on his fellow-archaeologists. Goodness, what's the time?

CHARLES. Quarter to six.

LAURA. I must go and make myself presentable. Oh dear, I'm terrified that he's going to propose at last. I shall *have* to accept him.

CHARLES. Why "have" to?

LAURA. He's kind. He's rich. He's devoted to me. The girls need a father. Every reason in the world.

CHARLES. Do you love him at all?

LAURA. I'm nearly forty. One doesn't fall in love at forty.

CHARLES. Doesn't one?

LAURA. No.

CHARLES. I'm not so sure.

LAURA. I am.

CHARLES. Are you?

LAURA. Well, I *think* I am.

CHARLES. Only think?

LAURA. Well—

> (*They are standing close together. The door-bell rings.* LAURA *jumps.*)

It's him. He's early.

CHARLES. Go on upstairs and do your face. I'll cope with him till you make your entrance—madam.

> (*She runs upstairs and he proceeds to the door and opens it.* EDWARD *stands there. He carries a large bunch of flowers.*)

EDWARD (*entering*). Evening, Charles.

CHARLES. Good evening, sir.

EDWARD. Mrs. Pemberton in?

CHARLES. Madam will be down in a moment, sir. Your coat, sir.

> (*He takes* EDWARD'S *coat.* EDWARD *still clutches the flowers.* CHARLES *goes out into the kitchen and returns with a decanter of sherry.*)

Sherry, sir?

EDWARD. Thank you. (*Looking about him.*) Well, you've certainly made a difference to this room, Charles. It's so tidy I hardly recognize it.

CHARLES. Indeed, sir? (*Giving him a glass.*)

EDWARD. I don't know if Mrs. Pemberton's told you I'm losing my housekeeper—I've had her for fifteen years—I shall be absolutely lost without her.

CHARLES. I'm so sorry, sir.

EDWARD. Do you know Cambridge at all?

CHARLES. I've been there, sir.

EDWARD. Very pleasant place to live.

CHARLES. I'm sure it is, sir.

EDWARD. I have a flat at King's Parade at the moment, but there's a house in the Queen's Road that I'm—er—interested in.

CHARLES. That's on the Backs, isn't it, sir?

EDWARD. Yes, looks right across to King's College Chapel. It's not a big house—just three reception rooms, five bedrooms and an excellent staff flat. Oh, and a kitchen of course—a first-class modern kitchen.

CHARLES. Very important, sir.

EDWARD. I expect you find the kitchen here not quite what you're accustomed to, eh?

CHARLES. It is rather cramped, sir.

EDWARD. The Queen's Road kitchen is stainless steel and enamel units—actually it's the only room in the house I should leave as it is. The rest of the décor is quite horrible, but the man's a scientist and you know what *they* are. (*He shudders slightly.*)

(LAURA *appears on the staircase.*)

LAURA. Hullo, Edward.

(CHARLES *goes into the kitchen, shutting the door.*)

EDWARD. Hello, my dear. (*He hands her the flowers.*)

LAURA. Aren't they gorgeous! Thank you so much. I'll give them to Charles to put in water and I'll arrange them afterwards.

(*She opens the kitchen door and hands in the flowers to* CHARLES.)

Put these in the sink, will you, Charles, and I'll see to them later. (*She shuts the kitchen door. To* EDWARD.) Well, and what are you doing in London? I thought you weren't coming up this week.

EDWARD. I had to see my publisher.

LAURA. What news of Mrs. Sandham?

EDWARD. It's quite definite. She insists on marrying the fellow—she says she's in love with him.

LAURA. But she must be fifty!

Y.O.S.—D

EDWARD (*hurt*). It's quite possible to be in love at fifty, you know, Laura.

LAURA. Is it?

EDWARD (*looking at her with meaning*). Quite possible.

LAURA (*hastily*). Do have some more sherry—I hope it isn't too dry, or do you like it dry, I forget?

EDWARD. No, thank you, Laura.

LAURA (*interrupting*). Caroline ought to be back at any minute. She's gone for a walk and—

EDWARD (*interrupting*). Laura.

LAURA. Yes, Edward.

EDWARD. How long have we known each other?

LAURA. It must be nearly twenty years.

EDWARD. I thought that first evening that you were the most enchanting person I had ever met and—

LAURA (*interrupting*). *Did* you, Edward? How very sweet of you. Now you *must* have another glass of sherry while I go and arrange your beautiful flowers. I won't be long. I'll—

EDWARD (*interrupting*). Laura, will you kindly not interrupt.

LAURA. Well, you're interrupting, too.

EDWARD. I've something I wish to say to you.

LAURA (*realizing she cannot escape*). Yes, Edward.

EDWARD. I want to tell you that I have loved you for twenty years.

LAURA. Edward!

EDWARD. I know you don't care for me in the same way, my dear, but I venture to think that you are fond of me.

LAURA. Oh, yes, Edward—very!

EDWARD. Will you marry me, Laura? I promise you I will do everything in my power to make you and the girls happy. I swear you'll never regret it.

LAURA. It's—it's terribly sweet of you, Edward, but—but, well, are you quite sure that, well, that I'd suit you? Would your Cambridge friends like me?

EDWARD. They'd adore you.

LAURA. But, Edward—

EDWARD. Laura, please say "yes".

LAURA. Oh, Edward, I do want to say "yes", I do indeed, only—

EDWARD. Only what?

LAURA. You said I wasn't in love with you. I'm not, but I really am very fond of you. I wasn't really in love with George, either, but

I was terribly happy with him. I've always thought that perhaps
one day I would fall in love—that I'd meet the man who—

EDWARD. Yes.

LAURA. Have you ever been so crazy about anyone that just to see
them made your knees knock together?

EDWARD. Once. She was eighteen. I was nineteen.

LAURA. What happened?

EDWARD. I went up to Cambridge, she went to Paris. That was in
October. I saw her at a dance on Christmas Eve and couldn't imagine
how I'd ever even thought she was pretty.

LAURA. Oh, Edward, how sad.

EDWARD. That sort of thing doesn't last, Laura.

LAURA. No, I know it doesn't and I'm too old for it anyway, only I
can't help feeling that if I say "yes" to you I'm shutting the door on
it forever.

EDWARD. I've seen a house in Queen's Road, on the Backs. It's got
a large studio in the garden where the girls could entertain their
friends. I see Caroline as the toast of the Cambridge Film Society
and Julia as the star of the Arts Theatre.

LAURA. And—and the shop?

EDWARD. I noticed a small one to be let in Trinity Street—quite
reasonably, too.

LAURA. Oh, Edward, how sweet of you—you know how I love my
little shop.

EDWARD. I do, my dear.

LAURA. And you're quite sure you're sure?

EDWARD. Quite sure.

LAURA. I'm not at all a model housekeeper.

EDWARD. Oh, we can leave all that to Charles.

LAURA. To Charles . . .

EDWARD. Laura, my darling Laura, please say "yes".

LAURA. But Edward—

EDWARD. Say "yes".

LAURA. Yes—but—

EDWARD (interrupting). I didn't hear the second word. (He kisses her.)
My dear, dear Laura! I've been waiting for that for twenty years.

LAURA. Have you, Edward?

EDWARD. Ever since that evening at the Bristowes. You wore pink,
I remember.

LAURA. I wore green and had a very bad cold in the head.

EDWARD (*firmly*). You wore pink and had no trace of a cold in the head. Now, darling, let's get down to practicalities. I'll see about the house, and the shop, and I think we should aim at getting married as soon as possible because I shall probably have to go to Central America in the autumn.

LAURA. To dig?

EDWARD. Yes. Hawkins has found relics of some primitive civilization ante-dating the Mayas and he wants me to go out for the winter.

LAURA. The whole winter? Can I come, too?

EDWARD. It's a filthy climate, we'll be living in tents, there are snakes, mosquitoes and other jolly things, so certainly not.

LAURA. Do you ever find "relics of primitive civilizations" in countries which have good climates and good hotels?

EDWARD. Very rarely.

LAURA. There's a message in that somehow, if one could work it out.

EDWARD (*laughing and putting his arm round her*). I must go now, my darling. Guess who I'm meeting at the Garrick Club—Robert Ferrars. He's just back from America.

LAURA. Ask him if he remembers—no, it doesn't matter.

EDWARD. Shall I send the announcement to *The Times?*

LAURA. What d'you mean?

EDWARD (*smiling*). Well, it's usual when people get engaged to be married.

LAURA. Oh, *must* we—I mean—Oh, Edward, couldn't it just be a secret between us for a few days—till I've told the girls and, and everything? Please, darling—just till next week.

EDWARD. But, Laura—

LAURA (*interrupting*). Please.

EDWARD. Very well, my dear. But I'll set a time limit. I'll be up here on Saturday—a week today—with it already drafted and in my pocket. We'll have lunch, and after lunch I'll drop it into a letter box.

LAURA. Thank you, Edward. You see, I shall have to find the right moment to tell the girls and all that.

EDWARD. They won't object, will they?

LAURA. I hate to tell you, but I believe they've been betting on it for the past two years!

(EDWARD *laughs and crosses to the chair and picks up his coat.*)

I think they'll both be absolutely delighted.

EDWARD (*kissing her*). And I'm absolutely delighted, too. Good night, my dear. I'll ring up in the morning.

LAURA. Good-bye, Edward—dear.

(*He goes. She stands staring after him. The kitchen door opens and* CHARLES *appears.*)

CHARLES. About dinner, madam. Will Miss Julia—

LAURA. I've said "yes".

CHARLES. You're going to—?

LAURA. I'm going to marry him.

CHARLES. I hope you'll be very, very happy.

(*He holds out his hand and* LAURA *takes it. They stand hand in hand, with eyes locked. The telephone rings.* CHARLES *drops* LAURA'S *hand and crosses to answer it.*)

Yes? Yes, it is madam, yes. (*To* LAURA.) It's Mrs. Pemberton, Senior, madam, she wants to know—why, what's the matter?

LAURA (*sinking into a chair*). I don't know, but something very odd seems to be happening to my knees!

CURTAIN

ACT THREE

The same. It is morning a week later and filthily wet.

JULIA is standing in an attitude before the window.

JULIA. "Oh Romeo, Romeo, wherefore art thou Romeo?
Deny thy father and refuse thy name
And I'll no longer be a Capulet."

(CHARLES enters from the kitchen.)

CHARLES. If you're still hungry after all that breakfast, Miss Julia, there are some doughnuts on the kitchen table.

(He goes upstairs.)

JULIA *(shuddering)*. Doughnuts! *(She gazes after CHARLES.)*
"She never told her love,
But let concealment like a worm i' the bud
Feed on her damask cheek. She pined in secret,
And with a green and yellow melancholy—

(CAROLINE enters from the front door. She is wearing a dripping mackintosh and carries an umbrella—equally dripping—and a basket of vegetables. She ignores JULIA and goes into the kitchen.)

She sat like Patience on a monument
Smiling at grief."
(Doing Orsino's part.) "But died this sister of her love, my boy?"
(Doing Viola again.) "I am all the daughters
Of my father's house, and all the brothers too—
And yet I know not. Sir, shall I to this lady?"

CAROLINE *(coming out of the kitchen)*. Where's Mummy? I've some change for her.

JULIA. In her room. Caro, she's been a bit odd this last week, don't you think? You know, sort of not quite with us.

CAROLINE. I think she's facing an emotional crisis.

JULIA. When I have an emotional crisis I always get so terribly hungry. D'you feel like a doughnut?

CAROLINE *(shuddering)*. No!

JULIA. Well I think I do. *(Moving towards the kitchen.)* Don't go, Caro. *(She goes into the kitchen.)*

CAROLINE *(calling)*. What's your crisis? Have you deserted John Neville for John Stride?

JULIA (*emerging with doughnuts and dignity*). There *are* other men. Sure you won't have one? (*Indicating the doughnuts.*)

CAROLINE. Quite sure.

JULIA. I suppose Edward's what you mean by Mummy's emotional crisis. He has rather come to the boil this last week, hasn't he? I mean, he rings up every night and they talk for hours.

CAROLINE. Psychologically it would be the best thing in the world if she accepted him. It's not natural for a woman of her type to live a celibate life. Cassandra Thomas says—

JULIA (*interrupting*). She talks more bunk to the square yard—

CAROLINE (*ignoring this*). Cassandra says that it's a miracle that Mummy's frustrations haven't reacted very unfavourably on us.

JULIA. Well, they haven't and thank the lord that Mummy isn't like Cassandra's mamma—she's nothing but a painted whore of Babylon.

CAROLINE. Really, Julia! You know you go to the Old Vic too much.

JULIA. That isn't the Vic, that's the Bible. Oh lord, if Mummy does marry Edward we'll have to go and live in Cambridge, won't we?

CAROLINE. You will. You'll probably have to go to school there.

JULIA. How long is it from London by train?

CAROLINE. About an hour and a half.

JULIA. Oh fiddle, that means I'll only be able to go to matinées.

CAROLINE. I might be able to put you up at the flat now and again.

JULIA. What d'you mean?

CAROLINE. Cassandra's probably going to Germany to work on Hans Doppleganger's new film. So I thought I'd take over her flat. It's frightfully cheap and I'd probably get someone to share it with me.

JULIA. I wonder if Mummy will . . .

CAROLINE. I hope so. After all, it's ten years since Daddy died.

JULIA. I wish I remembered him properly. I can just remember he was big, not very tall and gave off a terrific sort of warmth. He liked Edward, didn't he?

CAROLINE. They were great friends—that's why Daddy made him his executor.

JULIA. I like him, too, in a dim sort of way, don't you?

CAROLINE. He's emotionally immature, but he'll be kind to her and won't give in to her whims too easily. Mummy's a darling but she needs a firm hand.

JULIA. Charles likes him, too.

CAROLINE. Charles?

JULIA. Well, it's jolly important. After all if Mummy *does,* Charles will be coming to Cambridge, too.

CAROLINE. Oh, I'd rather thought . . . (*She pauses.*)

JULIA. What?

CAROLINE. Well, I'd rather thought that he might have preferred to stay in London and—er—free lance. I might have been able to arrange for him to do various people's flats . . .

JULIA. Well, the subject of Cambridge cropped up the other day—or rather I brought it up—and he said it was one of the most beautiful places in the world to live in.
"Would I were in Grantchester, in Grantchester,
Some it may be can get in touch
With Nature, there, or Earth or such . . ."

(CAROLINE *is now abstractedly eating the last doughnut.*)

(*She breaks off.*) I thought you didn't want any doughnuts!

CAROLINE (*munching*). You know, you get worse. Quoting's become a positive disease with you.

JULIA (*striking an attitude*). "Here lies Julia Miranda Pemberton who died of a surfeit of quotations." Never mind, Caro, when you've got Cassandra's flat you'll be spared much of my company.

CAROLINE. I may not get it. After all, it's probably not a very good idea. You see . . . (*She pauses.*)

JULIA. Yes?

CAROLINE. You see, Mummy might fuss a bit about me being on my own. Now, if Charles had been able to pop in and keep an eye on one . . .

JULIA. But you said you'd get someone to share with you. Mummy wouldn't fuss then. Particularly if it was someone revoltingly respectable like Alison Williams-Owen.

CAROLINE (*airily*). Alison's got a lover.

JULIA. No! Do tell!

CAROLINE. He's in the Foreign Office and they spent a week-end at Gleneagles together. She said it was zymotic.

JULIA. Well, get her to a nunnery!

CAROLINE. No, I could probably spend the odd night with Aunt Margaret or Grannie and come up to Cambridge for the week-ends —and for the holidays, of course.

JULIA. On the other hand Mummy may say "No".

CAROLINE. She may, but—

(CHARLES *appears down the staircase. He has taken off his apron and carries a suitcase and overcoat.*)

Are you going away for the week-end, Charles?

CHARLES. No, miss. No, the fact is that I'm leaving here. I'm very sorry but I've got another job and—

(*The* GIRLS *are staring at him open mouthed.*)

CAROLINE (*incredulously*). You're leaving?

JULIA. But you can't!

CHARLES. I don't want to, Miss Julia, but this other job offers me better prospects and—

CAROLINE (*interrupting*). Does Mother know?

CHARLES. Oh yes, miss. She advised me to snap up this other job at once as it were. I've managed to get a man to take my place here.

JULIA (*running to the foot of the stairs*). Mummy! Mummy!

CAROLINE. But, Charles—

CHARLES. Well, Miss Caroline, you did advise me to better myself.

(LAURA *appears at the head of the staircase.*)

LAURA. What's the matter?

JULIA. It's Charles—he says he's leaving us!

LAURA (*coming downstairs*). I'm afraid he is. He's got the offer of this very good job, so of course we can't stand in his way.

CAROLINE. But he can't leave just like this!

JULIA. "It is too rash, too unadvised, too sudden."

CAROLINE. What is the new job?

CHARLES (*glibly*). I am returning to Mr. Mallard as his personal secretary and companion.

JULIA. I don't believe you! I think you feel your weakness coming over you and are afraid it will upset us. But it won't. I haven't told a soul, as I promised, but if you'll let me break my word—I'm sure they'll understand.

CAROLINE. But I *do* understand! Charles told me.

JULIA. He told *you?*

CAROLINE. Of course. Goodness knows how *you* managed to find out.

JULIA. I didn't find out! He told me! That's why I put them away!

CAROLINE. You didn't put them away—I did!

JULIA. You didn't!

CAROLINE. But I *did!*

CHARLES (*interrupting soothingly*). I think there may be some little misunderstanding.

LAURA (*overlapping*). Yes, I'm sure there's—
  (*The* GIRLS *take no notice but stand glaring at each other.*)
JULIA. Caroline Mary Pemberton, you're a filthy liar!
CAROLINE. I'm not—you are!
JULIA. I'm not!
CAROLINE. *I* took them and put them in my wardrobe!
LAURA. Darlings, please!
JULIA (*ignoring* LAURA). You didn't! I took them and put them in
  my desk, except for the ashtray and that I had to leave—but I put
  it in the table drawer.
CHARLES. If you'd please let me explain—
CAROLINE. Mummy, I think Julia's gone mad!
JULIA. I haven't! I tell you I took them all except for the ashtray!
CAROLINE. Stark, raving mad!
JULIA. Stark, raving mad yourself!
CHARLES (*in stentorian tones*). Be quiet, you two!
  (*They both turn to him.*)
CAROLINE ⎫ (*simultaneously*). ⎧ But she must be raving—did you hear?
JULIA   ⎭   ⎩ Honestly, I think you ought to get a doctor!
CHARLES (*interrupting in even more stentorian tones*). Will you be quiet,
  you little idiots! (*They are checked by this.*) Now, listen, I have to
  apologize very humbly to both of you. When I told you I had a
  "weakness" I didn't tell you what it really was. I'm not a klepto-
  maniac, Miss Julia. I'm not an alcoholic, Miss Caroline. I'm just
  a congenital liar.
LAURA. Charles, I can't let you—
CHARLES (*silencing her with a look*). I can no more help lying than I can
  help breathing.
JULIA (*slowly*). You mean, you mean there wasn't one word of truth
  in all that about the little things?
CHARLES. Not one word.
CAROLINE. And you don't—you don't take little nips?
CHARLES. Certainly not to that extent.
JULIA. But why— (*She pauses.*) Why?
CHARLES. Why did I tell you those particular lies? Because I was
  playing for sympathy; because that's the sort of rotten despicable
  thing I do to people who've been kind to me. (*We realize that he is
  playing another role for all he is worth.*) Because I'm that old fashioned
  thing, a cad and a waster. You're lucky to have found me out so
  soon.

LAURA. But, Charles—

CHARLES (*giving her another look*). All my life I've lied and cheated. And nobody and nothing can change me. I'll go lying and cheating to my grave—and laughing at those who've been fools enough to believe in me.

JULIA. I think you're the most horrible man I've ever met in my life!

(*She rushes past him upstairs.*)

LAURA. Julia, darling.

(*A door slam is the only reply.*)

Charles, I don't see why—

CAROLINE (*to* CHARLES). Have you been laughing at me?

CHARLES (*cheerfully*). Like a drain, Miss Caroline.

CAROLINE (*outraged*). Oh! Julia was quite right—you're horrible.

(*She stalks past him, goes up the stairs.* LAURA *makes a gesture after her, but* CHARLES *shakes his head.* CAROLINE'S *door slams.* CHARLES *breathes a sigh of relief.*)

LAURA. Now will you kindly explain why you thought it necessary to make yourself appear as a sort of monster?

CHARLES. There's a scene in an old play called "David Garrick" in which the hero pretends he is a villain to the girl he loves because he knows she will be better off with someone else, and can only learn to love that someone else if she is completely disillusioned about him.

LAURA. Well?

CHARLES. Those two dear girls were both suffering from a nice little schoolgirl crush upon me. All sorts of jealousy might have resulted. Now they will be happily united in discovering that I'm the most horrible man they've ever met.

LAURA. So you were being kind of altruistic?

CHARLES. Kind of.

LAURA. But you enjoyed playing the scene, didn't you?

CHARLES. Kind of.

LAURA. I know what your "weakness" really is—acting!

CHARLES. I'm afraid so.

LAURA. I knew from the first that you weren't an ordinary normal person.

CHARLES. Aren't we theatre people normal?

LAURA. No.

CHARLES. What about Julia—isn't she already one of us?

LAURA. Yes. I've no idea how it happened. I went to see Sir Laurence Olivier in "Othello" the night before she was born, but that was rather too late to be a proper pre-natal influence.

(*They both laugh and there is a slight pause.*)

CHARLES. Well, I ought to be going.

LAURA (*hastily*). Oh, you can't go without having a drink with me. Is the sherry in Caroline's wardrobe?

CHARLES. No, the kleptomaniac side of me removed it this morning. (*He goes into the kitchen and emerges with the sherry.*) I've put the casserole on for this evening very low, and there's plenty of cold stuff for the girls' lunch. You'll be out, won't you?

LAURA. Yes. Yes, Edward's coming up from Cambridge.

CHARLES (*briskly*). Berenger said this man Hopkins is one of his best— an ex-Marine in his sixties and a terrific martinet. Anyway, it won't be for long, will it?

LAURA. Why not? (*Taking a glass of sherry from him.*)

CHARLES. Well, you'll be going to live in Cambridge, won't you?

LAURA. Oh, yes.

CHARLES (*lifting his glass*). Your happiness!

LAURA (*lifting hers*). Yours! (*They drink.*) What are your plans, by the way? Are you going direct to another job?

CHARLES. No. I'm taking a week's grace. There are a lot of things I want to think over carefully, so this afternoon I'm going to take a Green Line bus somewhere out into the country and then walk west. I shall become a minor Hilaire Belloc character and stay in small pubs, drink a great deal of beer and live on bread and cheese.

LAURA. And then?

CHARLES. Well, then I don't honestly know. I may go back to Berenger, or I may not.

LAURA. You'll come and see us, won't you?

CHARLES. No.

LAURA. If it's because of the girls—

(*She stops as* JULIA *appears on the staircase in her mackintosh.*)

JULIA. Mummy, they're showing "Richard Three" at the Classic. I'm going round to Susan's to see if she'll come with me this afternoon.

LAURA. All right, darling. I thought you'd both seen it, though?

JULIA. I have ten times, but Susan only six and a half—she fainted during the coronation.

(*Ignoring* CHARLES, *she goes out, closing the front door behind her.*)

CHARLES. A very nice clean exit. She'll be all right.

LAURA. She looked miserable, poor sweet.

CHARLES. The winter of her discontent will soon be made glorious technicolour by three hours of John Neville and some Cadbury's Dairy Milk.

LAURA. What exactly are you playing now?

CHARLES. The cynic *malgré lui*.

LAURA. Are you never yourself?

CHARLES. Very rarely. It's a way of escape and as good as any. I think I might be always myself with—with the right audience.

LAURA. But you must have an audience?

CHARLES. Or perhaps I should have said with the right partner.

LAURA. After all, to an actor the audience is a sort of partner, isn't it? I mean, one can't do without the other.

CHARLES. I'm so sorry I'm going.

LAURA. Oh, so am I. Charles, listen, don't you think—

CHARLES. No.

LAURA. If you were only going back to the stage—Charles, why don't you give it just one more chance?

CHARLES. It's too late.

LAURA. It's not. How old are you?

CHARLES. Forty.

LAURA. But that's nothing. How old was—well, say Irving, when he made his first success?

CHARLES. I've no idea.

LAURA. Well then. What I mean is, he might have been forty.

CHARLES. You know, there are times when you are more like Julia than Julia herself.

LAURA. Am I?

CHARLES. Yes, also much younger and infinitely more confused.

LAURA. But, seriously, Charles—

(*She stops as* CAROLINE *appears on the staircase in her mackintosh.*)

CAROLINE. Mother, I'm going to have some coffee with Cassandra and see if she can come and see "The Modigliani Mystique" at the Curzon this afternoon.

LAURA. All right, darling.

CAROLINE. I may spend the night with her afterwards—I feel the need of a change of atmosphere.

(*Ignoring* CHARLES, *she goes out, closing the front door behind her.*)

CHARLES. That wasn't a bad exit, either. I begin to detect a distinctly theatrical streak in this "normal" family. Are you, by any chance, a repressed actress?

LAURA. Well, I played Cassius at school once, dressed in a sheet and a wreath of laurels picked from bushes in the school drive that smelt quite awful. I think that got it out of my system. But to return to you—

CHARLES. To return to me, I should be on my way.

LAURA. You know, I don't see why I should be the only one of the family who doesn't try to inspire you.

CHARLES. But you do inspire me.

LAURA. But I don't—or rather I haven't yet.

CHARLES. I think just knowing you might be an inspiration to—to anybody.

LAURA. But you aren't "anybody".

CHARLES. I'm just nobody—and I must go and catch my Green Line bus.

LAURA. But you haven't finished your sherry.

CHARLES. No more I have. (*He picks up his empty glass.*)

LAURA. Oh dear, how silly of me—you *have* finished it.

CHARLES. So I have.

LAURA. One for the Green Line?

CHARLES. Thank you.

LAURA (*chattily as she pours out the sherry*). What bus are you taking?

CHARLES. The first that comes that'll take me into the real country.

LAURA. Are you country-bred?

CHARLES. Country Rectory-bred.

LAURA. So am I! My father was Rector of Clever in Dorset.

CHARLES. And mine of Weldon-on-the-Wall in Northumberland.

LAURA. I wonder if they knew each other. You know that really seems to bring us very close together.

CHARLES. Yes, it does, doesn't it?

(*They are in fact very close together, but the telephone rings.* CHARLES *crosses and lifts the receiver.*)

Yes. Yes, sir. (*To* LAURA.) Mr. Llewellyn, madam.

LAURA (*at telephone*). Hello, Edward. Yes. Yes, I'll be ready. (*Unconvincingly.*) Oh, that'll be lovely. No, nothing's the matter. Yes, I'll be ready. (*She sees* CHARLES *picking up his suitcase.*) Stop! (*To telephone.*) No, Edward, I wasn't speaking to you. Yes. Yes. In ten minutes. (*She hangs up.*) Charles, it's simply pelting still—you'll get soaked.

CHARLES. I don't mind the rain.

LAURA. Have you an umbrella?

CHARLES. No.

LAURA. I have. I have two, actually.

CHARLES. Have you?

LAURA. Yes—yes—I—I could lend you one.

CHARLES (*tenderly*). Could you?

LAURA. Yes. I— (*She gulps and takes a grip on herself.*) What exactly were we discussing when the telephone rang?

CHARLES. I can't remember.

LAURA. I can. It was about probably having been childhood friends— we easily could have been. After all, if our fathers knew each other . . .

CHARLES (*smiling*). Did we establish that?

LAURA. Oh, they must have. Daddy was at Oxford with practically everybody.

CHARLES. My father went to Cambridge.

LAURA (*dashed*). Oh, well, they may have rowed against each other, or something. Did your father row?

CHARLES. No. He played chess.

LAURA (*triumphantly*). So did mine! They were probably the greatest friends. All those terrible gambits—you know, S.P.Q.R. to K. four. They probably played it by post for years!

(*There is a ring at the front door.* LAURA *jumps.*)

CHARLES (*reassuringly*). I ordered some extra milk.

(*He goes to the door and opens it.* MRS. PEMBERTON *stands on the threshold.*)

MRS. P. (*entering*). Of all the filthy days!

LAURA. Darling, how nice to see you! What are you doing up here on a day like this?

MRS. P. My daughter Margaret's gone mad. (*To* CHARLES, *who is taking her mackintosh and umbrella.*) Charles, I've only a minute, but I'd adore a cup of really good strong hot coffee.

CHARLES. Certainly, madam.

(*He goes into the kitchen.*)

LAURA. Margaret's gone mad?

MRS. P. She's going to get married.

LAURA. But, Mama-in-law, surely—

MRS. P. She's fifty.

LAURA. I've been told one can still be in love at that age.

MRS. P. He's thirty-five and an American.

LAURA. Is he rich?

MRS. P. No, he's the one that isn't.

LAURA. But, if she's in love with him?

MRS. P. Rubbish! She just wants something to look after, now that
wretched little peke is dead.

LAURA. I can't understand why she never married.

MRS. P. Because, quite frankly, Edward Llewellyn never looked at
her after you appeared upon the scene.

LAURA. I didn't know . . .

MRS. P. He'd probably never have looked at her anyway.

LAURA. Isn't it an unfair world? A loves B and B only cares for C
and C only lives for a word from A. It's like some nightmare
problem in geometry. Are you going to try and prevent her from
marrying this man?

MRS. P. I'm going to prevent her making a fool of herself.

LAURA. Poor Margaret. It must be wonderful to make a fool of
yourself just once in your life.

MRS. P. Laura, what are you talking about? (*Indicating the sherry.*)
A bit early for that, isn't it? I was really very seriously worried
about you the other evening. Did Edward notice anything?

LAURA. I don't think so.

MRS. P. How is he?

LAURA. All right. I'm having lunch with him today.

MRS. P. What are the girls doing? I'm not seeing Margaret till half
past three so, if they like, I'll give them lunch at Veccio's in Vicarage
Place.

LAURA. They'd adore that.

                    (CHARLES *enters with coffee.*)

MRS. P. Thank you.

CHARLES (*to* LAURA). For you, madam?

LAURA. No, I'll have a glass— (*She catches* MRS. PEMBERTON'S *eye and
capitulates.*) Yes, please.

MRS. P. I'll just look in at the shop to see if there are any letters,
go and cash a cheque at the Book Shop, do a few chores and be at
Veccio's at half past twelve. Where are the girls?

LAURA. Out seeing various chums about various plans for the after-
noon. They ought to be back soon.
CHARLES (*having poured and handed the coffee*). Will that be all, madam?
LAURA. Yes, thank you.
> (*He moves towards the door and she realizes he means to go.*)

I mean, no—there are several things I want to talk to you about—
the washing machine's gone all broody and—
CHARLES. Very good, madam.
> (*He goes into the kitchen and closes the door.*)

MRS. P. Are you quite well, Laura? You seem so flustered.
LAURA. I'm not in the least flustered.
MRS. P. Are you sure you haven't a temperature?
LAURA. I'm perfectly all right.
MRS. P. Well, have a nice relaxing lunch with Edward and forget
all your worries. By the way, did you have your "heart to heart"
with Charles?
LAURA. Yes. He's going.
MRS. P. What?
LAURA. Oh, he's not a crook or anything like that. He—well—he's
just got a better job, that's all. Anyway, I've got another coming
this afternoon.
MRS. P. Is he leaving *today?*
LAURA (*in a small voice*). Yes.
MRS. P. (*looking at her sharply*). Well, I'm sure it's all for the best.
You know I said he reminded me of Archdeacon Busvine? Well,
what I didn't tell you was that he ran away with the wife of one of
the Rural Deans, was unfrocked—or ungaitered or whatever they
do to them—and ended up on the stage! There was a terrible
scandal. Well, I must go. My love to Edward. (*She picks up her
mackintosh and* LAURA *helps her into it.*) I've been praying for rain for
my tomato plants for weeks past, but I do think the Almighty has
rather overdone His answer. Good-bye, my dear. Tell the girls
not to be late. Give my love to Edward. Bye.
LAURA. Bye, darling. Don't be too hard on Margaret.
MRS. P. Sometimes I wish that men had never been invented.
> (*She goes out, closing the door behind her.* LAURA *stands for a
> moment thinking. Then she gets an inspiration. She crosses to the
> kitchen door and opens it.*)

LAURA. Charles?

(*She goes back into the living-room.* CHARLES *enters from the kitchen.*)

CHARLES. This time I really must—

LAURA (*interrupting*). Charles, I've just realized I've been terribly remiss. You can't go without a reference—you know, like the one old Sir General Thing gave you—only this time it'll be genuine.

CHARLES. I think I'd rather like to have a reference from you.

LAURA. There's no "like" about it—you *must* have one. If I didn't give you one I'd probably be going against your Union or the G.L.C. or something like that. (*Rummaging in her desk.*) What do you want me to say? I've never written a reference before, so you'll have to tell me. (*Preparing to write.*) What do I call you?

CHARLES. Just Charles.

LAURA. Not Mr. Selby?

CHARLES. Just Charles.

LAURA. Just Charles?

CHARLES (*firmly*). Just Charles.

LAURA (*writing*). Just Charles. Oh, how silly of me, I mean, Charles. (*Scratching out.*) This will have to be only a rough draft. Well, what do I say?

CHARLES. Say I'm honest—except for a penchant for wrist watches.

LAURA (*writing*). "Is honest."

CHARLES. Sober—except for a predilection for little nips.

LAURA (*writing*). "Little nips"—bother! (*Scratching out and writing.*) "Sober."

CHARLES. And extremely industrious.

LAURA (*writing*). "Extremely industrious." Anything more? Oughtn't I to say you've given me complete satisfaction?

CHARLES. I only wish I had.

LAURA (*turning*). But you have! You've been wonderful. I've never been so satisfied. Why, even Nannie—

(*The front door opens and* JULIA *enters.*)

JULIA. That's O.K. with Susan.

LAURA. Grannie's been here. She wants you and Caroline to lunch with her at Veccio's.

JULIA. Oh, good.

LAURA. At twelve-thirty sharp. And put on your green jersey and cap.

JULIA. O.K. (*She looks rather pointedly at* CHARLES *but does not speak.*)

LAURA (*hastily*). I'm writing a reference for Charles.

JULIA. I hope you're telling the truth.

LAURA. Indeed I am.

JULIA. I'm sorry I said you were the most horrible man I'd ever met in my life, Charles.

CHARLES. That's all right, Miss Julia—I probably am.

JULIA. You see, I haven't met many men, but I was thinking just now about Iago and Angelo and Iachimo, and in comparison with them— well, you're not *so* bad.

CHARLES. Thank you, Miss Julia.

JULIA. Good-bye. (*She begins to go upstairs.*)

CHARLES. "I thank thee for thy mercy, gentle lady."

JULIA (*automatically*). "The quality of mercy is not strained, it droppeth as the gentle rain from Heaven upon the place beneath. It is twice blessed. It blesseth him that gives." (*She hesitates.*)

CHARLES (*prompting*). "And him that takes".

JULIA. "'tis mightier in the mightiest. It becomes the throne'd monarch . . ."

(*She disappears from view.*)

LAURA. Well, where were we?

CHARLES. You were just about to sign my reference.

LAURA. You're sure there's nothing I ought to add to it?

CHARLES. Just your name.

LAURA (*writing*). "Laura Amelia Pemberton".

CHARLES. Amelia!

LAURA. I know. Isn't it ridiculous?

CHARLES. No, it's enchanting. It suits you. Amelia . . . (*He takes the piece of paper.*) Thank you. I'll always treasure this as the most beautiful reference I've ever had or am ever likely to have.

LAURA. Will you?

CHARLES. Even if I rise in the social scale and my references become called testimonials.

LAURA. Well, I suppose . . .

CHARLES. Yes, I suppose. Hell, I don't want—

(*The front door opens, they both jump and* CHARLES *drops his reference without realizing it, and* CAROLINE *appears.*)

CAROLINE. I've organized that with Cassandra.

LAURA. Oh, good—you and Julia are having lunch with Grannie at half past twelve at Veccio's.

CAROLINE. Can I borrow a hat?

LAURA. Caroline!

CAROLINE. I've decided that in order to be a good citizen I must be more tolerant of Grannie's bourgeois principles. (*To* CHARLES.) Why haven't you gone?

CHARLES. Your mother has been giving me some good advice, miss.

CAROLINE. I hope you'll profit from it. I'm not angry with you any more, Charles—I just despise you utterly.

CHARLES (*meekly*). I quite understand, Miss Caroline.

CAROLINE. It is as if you had never existed.

(*She disappears up the stairs.*)

CHARLES. Well, this time I—

LAURA (*vivaciously*). What were we talking about just now? I *know* there was something I wanted to say to you—what was it now?

CHARLES. Good-bye.

LAURA. Good-bye?

CHARLES. Good-bye.

(*He turns, picks up his suitcase and goes to the front door.* LAURA *makes as if to call after him but checks herself. At the door* CHARLES *turns, his hand on the handle.*)

Good-bye, Amelia. (*He bows.*) Always your obedient servant.

LAURA. Charles!

(*For an instant it looks as if they are going to fly into each other's arms, but* CHARLES *takes a grip on himself and opens the door.* EDWARD *stands on the threshold.*)

EDWARD. Morning, Charles. Disgusting day, isn't it? (*He notices* CHARLES' *suitcase.*) Off for the weekend?

CHARLES. Yes, sir.

EDWARD (*entering*). Well, my dear.

(*As* EDWARD *comes into the room,* CHARLES *slips out of it, closing the door behind him.*)

LAURA. Hello, Edward.

EDWARD. What's the matter? You look upset. (*Kisses her.*)

LAURA. I'm all right—it's just such a filthy morning.

EDWARD. You need some sunshine. What do you say to a honeymoon at Portofino?

LAURA (*wistfully*). It sounds lovely.

EDWARD (*not noticing her tone*). Robert Ferrars has a villa there and he's offered it to us. I particularly want to go to Italy for several

reasons. I'm thinking of writing one of my thrillers about a family
of twentieth century Borgias who are unmasked, as we say in the
detection trade, by a visiting archaeologist and his lovely bride.
(*He notices her abstraction.*) You *are* upset!

LAURA (*pulling herself together*). No I'm not—honestly!

EDWARD. And you're not ready. I had a feeling you wouldn't be, so
I booked our table for one-fifteen.

LAURA. That was very thoughtful of you. I *meant* to be ready. I've
bought a new pink hat, too.

EDWARD. Bless you. What do the girls say?

LAURA. I haven't told them, actually. I thought perhaps—well, we
might tell them together tonight.

EDWARD. As you wish, my dear. (*He taps his breast pocket.*) I have it
written out here all ready to post.

LAURA. Well, I'd better go and put on a face to suit the hat.

(*She moves towards the staircase.*)

EDWARD. Ferrars sends you his regards. He's an extraordinary fellow
—completely disorganized like all his kind. Just imagine—he
starts rehearsing a new play on Monday and one of the leading
parts isn't cast yet. He's looking for some chap he saw in Melbourne
years ago who he says is the only person who can play it properly—
why, Laura what is it?

LAURA (*her face blazing with excitement*). Did he tell you the man's name?

EDWARD. No, I don't think so. Wait a minute. No.

LAURA (*almost shaking him*). Try and remember!

EDWARD. Darling, what does it matter?

LAURA. It matters terribly!

EDWARD. Laura, what are you in such a state about?

LAURA. Try and remember—please try and remember.

EDWARD. Laura dear—

LAURA (*interrupting*). Was it Selby?

EDWARD. Yes . . . yes, I believe it was.

LAURA (*collapsing on to sofa*). I *said* the chance was bound to come some
time! Whee!

EDWARD. Laura! What is it? I've never seen you like this before!

LAURA. I've never been like this before!

EDWARD. If it were anyone else I'd say they were drunk.

LAURA. I suppose I am in a sort of way.

EDWARD. What on earth does this man mean to you? Do you know
him?

LAURA. Yes, I . . . (*She pauses.*) Oh, Edward, I'm so sorry. I expect you think I'm crazy.

EDWARD. No, my dear. I think you're very overtired and not quite yourself. It wouldn't be a bad idea to see your doctor, and it wouldn't be a bad idea if he suggested a week in a nursing-home somewhere. You've been overworking for years with no one to help you, so no wonder you're nervy.

LAURA. Oh, Edward, you're sweet, really you are!

EDWARD. Thank you, my dear—and we'll leave the mystery of this man Selby till you want to tell me about it—if there's anything to tell.

LAURA. Edward, I can't marry you.

EDWARD. Darling, you're going to—there's nothing more to be said.

LAURA. But there is—lots.

EDWARD. Laura, we went through all this last week.

LAURA. But we didn't—

EDWARD (*interrupting*). You promised to marry me, and I'm sure you're the last person in the world to break her word or cause anyone unnecessary pain.

LAURA. Perhaps I'm not the person you think I am at all.

EDWARD. My dear Laura, I've known you for twenty years!

LAURA. You *think* you've known me. You think I'm a nice, ordinary, fairly amusing, fairly good-looking—

EDWARD (*interrupting*). *Very* good looking—

LAURA. —fairly intelligent woman. But I'm not. (*Dramatically.*) I'm a whited sepulchre!

EDWARD. Nonsense, my dear. Now, I suggest we cancel our table and have a little lunch here, and I'll ring up your doctor and—

LAURA. I hate to have to disillusion you, Edward.

EDWARD. Then don't try.

LAURA (*every inch a leading lady*). But I must. I can no longer conceal my weakness from you. It wouldn't be right.

EDWARD. Your weakness?

LAURA. Yes, my weakness.

EDWARD. Heart?

LAURA. Men!

EDWARD. Men?

LAURA. Yes. I suppose you could call it "heart" in a way.

EDWARD. Laura, what are you trying to say?

LAURA. It's the little ones I can't resist!

EDWARD. Little ones?

LAURA. I have a passion for Welshmen and jockeys.

EDWARD. Laura! Are you implying that—that you've had lovers?

LAURA. Hordes of them.

EDWARD. What?

LAURA. At least ten since Christmas.

EDWARD. Laura!

LAURA. So you see, it would be disastrous to marry someone like me
and take me to live in a place like Cambridge. Think of "Young
Woodley".

EDWARD. But it's impossible to believe that you—you of all people—
(*He pauses.*)

LAURA. The quiet ones like me are always the worst.

EDWARD. . . . that you of all people are a nymphomaniac!

LAURA. But I am! I'll be all right for a time, and then it'll suddenly
come over me.

EDWARD. Good God!

LAURA. I was tempted to marry you. You're a darling, Edward, and
famous and rich, but I suddenly realized today you were too fine a
person to cheat. Forgive me if you can, and forget me. (*She moves
off towards the foot of the stairs.*)

EDWARD. Laura, I am utterly bewildered: I don't know what to say!

LAURA. Don't try to say anything. Go back to Cambridge and thank
Heaven fasting for your deliverance.

EDWARD (*slowly*). But you *are* a different woman—everything you
say. You're not *my* Laura.

LAURA (*with a sad, sweet smile*). Your Laura never existed, Edward. She
was someone you imagined and to whom you gave my shape and
form. Poor Edward, how could you realize that I was rotten to the
core? (*She is over-playing rather badly now and* EDWARD *suddenly
bursts out laughing.*)

EDWARD. My dear, I'd no idea you were such a good actress. Though
why you've sprung it on me without warning, I've no idea. For a
moment you had me quite worried.

LAURA (*put out*). What d'you mean?

EDWARD. That song, "Maud, I said, I'm rotten to the core, and Maud
agreed". Beatrice Lillie, wasn't it?

LAURA. Oh dear.

EDWARD. But next time, give me warning.

LAURA. There won't be a next time, Edward.

EDWARD. Now, Laura—

LAURA (*interrupting*). Don't you see, in my muddled way I was trying to make it easier for you—I thought that if you imagined I was a thorough bad lot, you wouldn't mind breaking it off. So I can't be such a good actress after all. A really good one would have convinced you that I was a raving nympho.

EDWARD. But Laura, last week you—

LAURA (*interrupting*). Last week was last week. Oh, Edward, I'm dreadfully sorry. I *hate* hurting you—but you remember about me saying that I'd never been really properly in love?

EDWARD. I remember your saying something, but—

LAURA (*interrupting*). Well, I am now. That's why I can't marry you.

EDWARD (*slowly*). You're in love? (LAURA *nods*.) This man Selby? (LAURA *nods again*.) An actor? (*She nods once more*.) Did you know him when you said—when you said you'd marry me?

LAURA. Yes, but I didn't realize— (*She falters*.)

EDWARD. That you were in love with him?

LAURA. No. I've guessed it and tried to pretend it was only—only physical attraction, but just now—when you were being so sweet to me about my being overtired and needing a rest, I realized that there was no rest for me anywhere in this world unless I was with him.

EDWARD. I see. (*He moves towards the door*.)

LAURA. Oh, Edward, I feel too *awful*—I'm so terribly sorry.

EDWARD. That's all right, my dear. These things happen. Does he—does he care for you?

LAURA. I don't know. No, I don't suppose he does or he wouldn't have gone away without—but that's not the point, I'm afraid. All I know is that I—I love him.

(EDWARD *picks up his coat and turns, his hand on the door*.)

EDWARD. Good-bye, Laura.

LAURA. Good-bye.

EDWARD. Don't worry too much about me, my dear. I shall be all right. I love my work, and I'm successful at it, which is a great compensation.

LAURA (*from her heart*). If only you hadn't lost Mrs. Sandham!

EDWARD. I hadn't an opportunity to tell you. Mrs. Sandham has been jilted, too. She's coming back.

(*He smiles and goes out, closing the door behind him. She stands for a moment, and then runs across the room to the telephone, takes up the directory, looks up a number, picks up receiver and dials*.)

LAURA (*at telephone*). Can I speak to Sir Robert Ferrars, please. Mrs. Pemberton. . . . Hello! Sir Robert? Laura Pemberton here. Yes, indeed. Yes, it must be at least five years. . . . Yes, we're all very well, thank you. . . . Yes, he's just told me . . . very exciting . . . wouldn't George have been thrilled? Yes . . . er, what I really rang you about was because Edward said you were looking for an actor called Charles Selby. . . . Yes. . . . Yes, I do. . . . Yes. . . . He must have been jolly good for you to remember him all this time. . . . Yes. . . . Yes, I'm sure it's the only way to cast a play. . . . Yes. . . . Shall I tell him to get in touch with you? Before Monday? Yes. . . . Yes, I quite see that you'll have to take someone else if he doesn't. . . . Yes. . . . I'll get in touch with him right away. . . . Yes. . . . Oh, I'd adore to come to the first night. . . . Thank you so much . . . that would be wonderful. . . . Good-bye. (*She hangs up and then immediately dials another number.*) Hello? three-seven-three seven-four-naught-four? Mr. Selby, please. He's left? But he said he was going back to pack. . . . Oh, he's packed and gone already? I see. Could I have his address, please. He didn't leave one? Do you know anyone who would know? Have you Mr. Mallard's number? He is in New York? Yes. . . . No, thank you . . . (*She hangs up.*)

   (*She stands disconsolate, sighs, crosses to the window, opens it. Shuts it. Wanders back to the telephone. Looks at it. Crosses to fireplace, turns back to telephone and stands looking at it. Picks it up. Puts it down and crossing to the sofa, buries her face in her hands. The front door opens. She looks up.* CHARLES *stands there.*)
Charles!

CHARLES. I thought you'd have gone out to lunch. I left my reference behind me and I couldn't—

LAURA (*running to him*). Thank God! Charles, you must ring Robert Ferrars at once!

CHARLES. Robert Ferrars?

LAURA. Yes, he's been looking for you everywhere! He wants you to be in his new play—isn't it wonderful? It's your chance at last!

CHARLES. I don't understand—Robert Ferrars looking for *me?*

LAURA. Yes, he remembered you in that play in Melbourne—think of it. You must have been good!

CHARLES. He can't be looking for me.

LAURA. But he *is!* I've just been speaking to him. You must ring him up at once. I'll get him for you.

(She hurries to the telephone and starts to dial.)

CHARLES. But this is the most fantastic—

LAURA *(at telephone)*. Hello? Can I speak to Sir Robert Ferrars, please? Mr. Charles Selby! Thank you.

> *(She holds the receiver over to* CHARLES, *who takes it in a dazed way. As he talks the sun comes out and lights up the room like the best amber flood.)*

CHARLES. Hello: Yes, Charles Selby speaking. . . . Yes. . . . Yes, a long time ago. . . . That's very nice of you. . . . Yes, Mrs. Pemberton's just told me. . . . Yes. . . . No, I'm not at the moment. . . . Yes. . . . But don't you want me to read for you? . . . Yes. . . . On Monday? Yes. . . . Yes, I'll be there. . . . Good-bye. *(He hangs up and turns to* LAURA. *He still looks dazed.)* He wants me for quite a good part—he's mad—I shan't be able to play it.

LAURA. What do you mean?

CHARLES. What I say. Maybe I wasn't a bad actor years ago but I'm no good any more.

LAURA. How d'you know?

CHARLES. Because if they're really good, actors get somewhere by the time they're forty. No, I'll write to Ferrars and tell him that I've retired.

LAURA. You'll do no such thing!

CHARLES. I must. It wouldn't be fair on him.

LAURA. So you're going to try and turn down the chance of your life just because you're afraid? Charles, are you a man or a mouse?

CHARLES. Merely a rat.

LAURA. Well, you're not going to! I'm not going to let you!

CHARLES. Please try to understand. . . . I *am* afraid. I've waited for this for too long and now it's come too late to help me. No, I must write to him and take my bag and go. I would have gone earlier only I felt I couldn't go without my reference. I want to keep it always to remind me—not that I shall need reminding, but— *(He looks around him, sees the sheet of paper lying on the floor and picks it up.)* Here it is. Well— *(He turns back to* LAURA, *sees she is standing quite still—and crying.)* My darling, what is it?

LAURA. You're being such a b-bloody fool!

CHARLES. Don't cry—please.

LAURA. It's your fault—I'm so terribly disappointed!

CHARLES. I'm sorry. I didn't realize you'd be so interested.

(*He moves towards her. She looks away.*)

LAURA. Of course I'm interested. Robert had asked me to the First
Night. I was going to take Julia.

CHARLES. Not your fiancé?

LAURA. I haven't g-got one.

CHARLES. What?

LAURA. I—I jilted him—this morning.

CHARLES. Why?

           (*He moves closer. She avoids his eyes.*)   ·

LAURA. That's my business.

CHARLES. Why did you jilt him?

LAURA (*rounding on him*). You've no right to ask me that—any more
than you've a right to call me your darling!

CHARLES. I know I've no right to call you my darling.

LAURA. Then why did you do it?

CHARLES. Because you are.

LAURA. Thank God! (*She flings her arms around his neck, he puts his
around her and they kiss passionately.*)

CHARLES (*coming up for air*). We're crazy, my sweet—I adore you but
I've nothing to offer you.

LAURA. Don't be idiotic. You're going to make a terrific success in
Robert's play and I can keep on my dear little shop as a sideline.
I've got it all planned.

CHARLES. But if the play fails?

LAURA. There's always "Service for ladies".

    He laughs and they kiss passionately. Suddenly CHARLES' *knees
begin unmistakably to knock together. . . . And* CAROLINE *and*
JULIA, *coming down the stairs dressed for lunch with their grandmother,
stand rooted to the spot in amazement at the spectacle, as*

THE CURTAIN FALLS.

PROPERTY LIST

ACT I, SCENE I

SETTING ON STAGE

The place is in a general state of untidiness.

On black Louis work table D.R.
Two magazines

On mantelpiece R.
Quantity of bills and papers behind small statues
Packet of ten cigarettes
Box of matches

On bureau
Complete untidiness

Around bureau
Three pieces of paper

On Sheraton chair
Form

Below velvet chair D.R.
One pair of nylons
One ladies' jumper

On glass show case L. *of armchair* R.
Cigarette box with contents
Table lighter (practical)
Glass ashtray
Box of matches

On Sheraton two-drawer occasional table, R. *of settee*
Pop-up pad
Silver match box
Silver ashtray
Table lighter (practical)
Small pencil
Telephone with long lead between handphone and machine: the lead is
     twisted badly

Behind the cushion L. *on settee*
A ladies' apron

On modern table, front of settee
Piles of magazines
Two glass ashtrays
The Times

On banister
A coat and several other garments

Around the settee
Magazines
On settee
Magazines
On two-tier mahogany oval occasional table back L.
Statue
Glass ashtray
On half-circular occasional table back of settee
Silver tray: *on it:*
Whisky decanter, sherry decanter, soda syphon, three whisky tumblers, three sherry glasses
On Lyre coffee table D.L.
Several magazines

SETTING OFF C.

Act I, Scene 1	Two full carrier bags and a basket with a marrow
	One full shopping basket
	One gilted clock worth twelve pounds (antique)
	Gentleman's suitcase
Scene 2	String bag full of groceries and french loaf

SETTING OFF U.L.

Act I, Scene 1	Green apron for gentleman
Scene 2	Letters stamped and addressed
	Antique catalogue

SETTING OFF D.L.

Act I, Scene 1	Dish cloth
	Kettle with a little hot water
	Duster (set in apron after first exit of Charles to kitchen)
	Tray (silver): *on it:*
	Teapot (full), jug with milk, bowl with sugar (lumps), three cups and saucers with spoons
Scene 2	Trolly: *on it:*
	Teapot (full), jug with milk, sideplates, paper napkins, two cups and saucers with spoons, bowl with sugar, tomato sandwiches on plate
	Silver tray: *on it:*
	Two cups and saucers with spoons, jug with milk, plate of tomato sandwiches, bowl with sugar lumps (empty space in top R.H. corner)
	Teapot (full) to follow
	Silver tray: *on it:*
	Sherry decanter, whisky decanter, soda syphon, three whisky tumblers, three sherry glasses

SETTING FOR ACT I, SCENE 2

Place is generally tidied up to look spick and span.

Strike
All magazines
Clock from mantelpiece
Kettle from D.L.
Clothes from banister
Papers from mantelpiece
Papers from bureau

Set: on modern table front settee
Two good fashion magazines
On two-tier mahogany oval occasional table
Vase with flowers

Move
Statue on two-tier mahogany oval occasional table to Lyre coffee table

ACT II

Strike
All small articles from:
    Glass show table, modern shelves, mantelpiece

Move
Lighter, matches to drawer in Sheraton table
Candlesticks to C. of mantelpiece

Strike
Drinks to off D.L.
Antique catalogue from velvet armchair

Set
Caroline coat: off U.L.

Set off C.
Case for carrying china
Handbag: *in it:*
    A Nantgarw coffee cup
    A large bouquet of flowers

Set off U.L.
Black bag: *in it:*
    A scrap of paper
    Check: Caroline's coat

Set off D.L.
Aspirin in a bottle
Mopping up cloth
Cup half full of coffee
Sherry bottle containing sherry
Tray: *on it:*
    Cup half full of coffee, jug of milk, bowl of sugar, pot of coffee

Tray: *on it:*
  Sherry decanter, whisky decanter (half full), whisky tumblers (three),
  sherry glasses (three), soda syphon

ACT III

Swop flowers over with statue.

Set on bureau bookcase
  Paper, pad, pen, ink, pencils, Biro, envelopes

Strike
  Black bag, coffee cup, aspirin

Set off C.
  Basket of vegetables
  Umbrella (wet): GRANNIE
  Umbrella (wet): CAROLINE

Set off D.L.
  Three doughnuts on plate
  Tray: *on it:*
    Coffee in pot, jug with milk, bowl of coloured sugar, two cups (one half
    full) with saucers and spoons
  Tray: *on it:*
    Sherry decanter, two sherry glasses, each half full

Personals

CHARLES
  Three references
  Notebook
  Pencil
  Key (practical)
  String bag (in coat pocket)
  Watch

GRANNIE
  Packet of cigarettes (Guards brand)
  Mackintosh (to be soaked in Act III)

CAROLINE
  Change
  Key (practical)

JULIA
  Key (practical)

LAURA
  Handbag: *in it:*
    Scrap of paper
    Key (practical)

FURNITURE LIST

(Measurements: length × breadth × height)

8 ft. long settee
Velvet armchair
5 ft. × 1 ft. 6 in. very low modern table
Black Sheraton occasional chair
Black Regency elbow chair
Black Louis work table: 1 ft. 9 in. × 1 ft. 2 in. × 2 ft. 4 in.
Lyre coffee table: 2 ft. × 1 ft. 2 in. × 1 ft. 10 in.
Glass show table: 2 ft. × 1 ft. 5 in. × 2 ft. 6 in.
Modern cane table: 2 ft. 7 in. square × 2 ft. 3 in.
Set of modern shelves: optional
Bookcase bureau: 3 ft. × 1 ft. 9 in.
Two tier mahogany oval occasional table: 2 ft. 2 in. × 1 ft. 9 in. × 2 ft. 5 in.
Sheraton two drawer occasional table: 1 ft. 7 in. × 1 ft. 4 in. × 2 ft. 6 in.
Three modern cane chairs
Half-circular occasional table: same height as back of settee. Diameter: 3 ft.
One trolley
Pair of Empire pedestals: optional
Mahogany pedestal: optional